# FIRE AT THE FOUNDING

Christian Clergy Laid Essential
Foundations for Liberty,
Righteousness, Morality, and
Just and Limited Government

## Thomas W. Jacobson

Foreword by D. James Kennedy

2ⁿᵈ Edition with Bible Study,
Discussion & Sermon Notes

WESTBOW
PRESS®
A DIVISION OF THOMAS NELSON
& ZONDERVAN

This book is a work of non-fiction. Unless otherwise noted, the author and the publisher make no explicit guarantees as to the accuracy of the information contained in this book.

WestBow Press books may be ordered through booksellers or by contacting:

WestBow Press
A Division of Thomas Nelson & Zondervan
1663 Liberty Drive
Bloomington, IN 47403
www.westbowpress.com
844-714-3454

**Fire At The Founding** is also available through the author's websites: www.GLCPublications.com.

Scripture quotations taken from the (NASB®) New American Standard Bible®, Copyright © 1960, 1971, 1977, 1995 by The Lockman Foundation. Used by permission. All rights reserved. www.lockman.org

ISBN: 979-8-3850-2443-8 (sc)
ISBN: 979-8-3850-3428-4 (hc)
ISBN: 979-8-3850-2444-5 (e)

Library of Congress Control Number: 2024908524

Print information available on the last page.

WestBow Press rev. date:   09/19/2024

**Rev. Jonathan Mayhew, 1750**: "It is hoped that but few will think the subject . . . improper . . . to be discoursed on in the pulpit, under a notion that this is *preaching politics*, instead of Christ. However, to remove all prejudices of this sort, I beg it may be remembered that 'all Scripture is profitable for doctrine, for reproof, for correction, for instruction in righteousness' (2 Timothy 3:16). Why, then, should not those parts of Scripture which relate to *civil government* be examined and explained from the desk, as well as others? Obedience to the civil magistrate is a Christian duty; and if so, why should not the nature, grounds, and extent of it be considered in a Christian assembly? Besides, if it be said that it is out of character for a Christian minister to meddle with such a subject, this censure will at last fall upon the holy apostles. They write upon it in their epistles to Christian churches; and surely it cannot be deemed either criminal or impertinent to attempt an explanation of their doctrine."

**Rev. Abraham Williams, 1762**: "Human Laws can't control the Mind. — The Rights of Conscience, are unalienable; inseparable from our Nature; — they ought not — they cannot possibly be given up to Society. Therefore *Religion, as it consists* in *right Sentiments, Affections*, and *Behaviour* towards God, — as it is chiefly *internal* and *private*, can be regulated only by God Himself."

**Rev. Samuel West, 1776**: "Unlimited submission and obedience is due to none but God alone. He has an absolute right to command; He alone has an uncontrollable sovereignty over us, because He alone is unchangeably good."

**Rev. Samuel West, 1776**: "(I)t is part of the work and business of a gospel minister to teach his hearers the duty they owe to magistrates. Let us, then, endeavor to explain the nature of their duty faithfully, and show them the difference between liberty and licentiousness; and, while we are animating them to oppose tyranny and arbitrary power, let us inculcate upon them the duty of yielding due obedience to lawful authority. In order to the right and faithful discharge of this part of our ministry, it is necessary that we should thoroughly study the law of nature, the rights of mankind, and the reciprocal duties of governors and governed. By this means we shall be able to guard them against the extremes of slavish submission to tyrants on one hand, and of sedition and licentiousness on the other. We may, I apprehend, attain a thorough acquaintance with the law of nature and the rights of mankind, while we remain ignorant of many technical terms of law."

**Rev. Samuel Stillman, D.D., 1779**: "Thus saith [Jesus] unto them, 'Render therefore unto Caesar the things that are Caesar's, and unto God the things that are God's' (Matthew 22:21). . . . I shall therefore proceed to apply this sacred passage to ourselves, in our present situation, by considering:

I.  What those duties are which the people owe to the civil magistrate.
II. The duties of the magistrate to the people. And then,
III. Endeavor to draw the line between the things that belong to Caesar, and those things that belong to God. . . ."

# ENDORSEMENTS

Thomas Jacobson has done yeoman's work in writing the second edition of Fire At The Founding. Thomas' book should be mandatory reading for every student of theology or practical ministry, particularly aspiring pastors. Fire At The Founding will help pastors today understand that the Pulpit was the vanguard of the political worldview that formed the freest, most prosperous, most beneficent, most prolific missionary-sending Republic in human history. But when many pastors and churches submitted to the unconstitutional 1954 Johnson Amendment, which was designed to silence the pulpits of America on critical matters of government and politics, they absolved themselves from their sacred duty to secure liberty to their own generation and to Posterity, and surrendered the Civil Society to the children of disobedience (Colossians 3:6). I pray that Thomas' book will be read by pastors across America, and jolt those who are asleep to awaken from their slumber and call their congregations into the fight for our Blessed Country.

– Rev. William Cook, Founder, America's Black Robe Regiment.

I am so excited to endorse this book to anyone who cares passionately about the state of the Church and our nation! As one who had to stand up against our governor in Colorado and keep our church doors open during the pandemic, I am well aware of the importance of using the pulpit to stimulate faith both from the Bible and from the U.S. Constitution. May this book fire you up with fresh love for Jesus and our nation!

– Dr. Steve Holt
Founder, Senior Pastor, The Road @ Chapel Hills,
Colorado Springs, CO
Founder, Worshipper Warrior Men's Ministry
Author of the best-selling book, *Worshipper and Warrior*

I am approaching my fourth decade in full-time ministry as the senior pastor within the same church. It wasn't until my 21st year of ministry that I learned about the profound and vital impact that pastors and clergy played in the founding of America. Thomas Jacobson has done an amazing job in his book, *Fire At The Founding*, through diligent research of rare and hard-to-find books, original documents, and the writings of our founders. You will discover the secret of their success in laying the solid foundations of the greatest nation in the history of the world. Psalm 11:3 asks the question, *"If the foundations be destroyed, what can the righteous do?"* My answer to that is: *get busy rebuilding them!* I believe the book that you hold in your hands will help you to do just that.

– Mark Cowart, Senior Pastor,
Church For All Nations, Colorado Springs, CO

# CONTENTS

# DEDICATION

The FIRE AT THE FOUNDING is dedicated to:

The bold and courageous clergy who laid righteous foundations for the United States, those who followed in their steps like Dr. D. James Kennedy, Rev. Bill Cook and America's Black Robe Regiment pastors, Dr. Steve Holt (my pastor), Pastor Mark Cowart, and those who will do likewise after reading this book.

The late Dr. Francis A. Schaeffer, who profoundly impacted my life, teaching me that the Word of God speaks to every area of life, that Jesus Christ is sovereign over all, and to think Biblically as a Christian.

My father, the Rev. Gerald D. Jacobson, who taught me much about the Living God and His ways, and who has been the greatest supporter of this and other works.

My brother, Col. (Ret.) Dr. Michael D. Jacobson, and his wife Susie, who walked the same journey as I, discovering God as Creator, Jesus as Savior, Lord and Friend, and the Bible as the foundation for truth for every area.

My son Gabriel and his beloved wife Tess and their daughter Owen Starr, and my son Seth and his future wife, and all our generations to come.

My friend and encourager, Stan John, and Global Life Campaign donors who made publishing this book possible.

**Other publication**: *Abortion Worldwide Report: 1 Century, 100 Nations, 1 Billion Babies. The History, Policies, and Sacred Accounting, and the Means to Restore Protection of Human Life*, by Thomas W. Jacobson and Wm. Robert Johnston (GLC Publications, 2018; new edition will be published in 2024).

# PREFACE

FIRE AT THE FOUNDING is built around a compilation of excerpts – priceless gold nuggets of truth and wisdom – from the writings, sermons and books of clergy during the 1700s, found primarily in the Rare Book Room of the United States Library of Congress. For years I was increasingly troubled by what I observed in our government, Congress, and across the nation that appeared to be the opposite of what I was discovering in original documents, and what our forefathers gave their lives to build. Therefore, I went to the Library of Congress to find the truth from original sources. I wanted to know what the American people during the founding generations believed and how they thought that enabled them to build the greatest nation in history. I discerned that if we did not rediscover and restore those foundations, the nation would continue to self-destruct.

In this second edition, at the end of each chapter, I have added a Bible study, questions for consideration or discussion, and sermon outlines.

In public schools, I received a false and contemptuous view of the people and history of the United States, particularly of the founding generations and Founding Fathers (who risked their lives to build something better for posterity). To me, there was little or nothing about my nation worth preserving.

After high school, I went to Bible college (1974-1976). Even though I was raised in a Christian family and in the church, and now had a Diploma of Biblical Studies, I still had no idea how to connect my faith or the Bible with anything beyond personal faith and the Church. Unethical practices by some at work, a lack of integrity and corruption of public officials, and the reality that I could be persuaded within five minutes that abortion was justified in particular situations, all bothered my conscience. Something was wrong, but I didn't know where to find the answers, where to find truth?

Then in 1982, I was traveling around Europe wondering if God was truly real, if He had any purpose for my life, and if my faith had any relevance to life here on earth? After two months of Eurail travel, I went to L'Abri in Switzerland to study under Dr. Francis A. Schaeffer. He enabled me to understand that the Bible speaks to every area of life, and the Lordship of Christ covers every area of authority, knowledge, education, government, history, and nations.

From L'Abri, I went to Regent University to study from a Biblical and Judeo-Christian foundation, and received my Master's degree in Public Policy (1983-1985). The relationships and education at L'Abri and Regent transformed my mind, worldview, and life, and taught me to think.

From 1985 through 1988, I worked for a Member of Congress, but the contrast between the truth I learned at L'Abri and Regent, and the reality and practice of our government, the ignorance and disregard for our *Constitution* or almost any limits of Federal authority, and the corrupt nature and objectives of so many in high office, troubled me greatly. Therefore in 1993-1994, I set aside a year to conduct research at the Library of Congress, including in the Rare Book Room. I researched how our Founding Fathers thought about rights of conscience, religious liberty, religion, government, public policy, and nations. There I discovered many writings of clergy, private leaders, and public leaders from the 1700s.

While conducting this research, I did not intentionally look for materials written by clergy, but the majority of books and documents I found were written by them. As I read from private leaders (e.g., Thomas Clap, Samuel Adams), and public leaders (e.g., George Washington, Benjamin Franklin, Thomas Jefferson, James Madison), I noticed they were declaring the same truths and principles that the preachers had already taught them, yet without quoting the Bible.

Thus, I discovered the great influence of the preachers, who were America's true Founding Fathers. They were often the most learned men. They studied the Bible for wisdom pertaining to matters affecting the community or nation, and had at least a good laymen's understanding of history, law, and nations. Within them was the FIRE of the Holy Spirit, the Word of God, Truth, and the Gospel of Jesus Christ, that taught and inspired the people, leaders, and officials of the American Colonies. The clergy prepared them to become a self-governing and free nation, and to face private and public challenges with the wisdom of God. Without them, there would have been no United States of America. The excerpts contained herein are a small representation of thousands of sermons and writings on numerous topics. Your mind and heart will be transformed as you read the gold nuggets of wisdom I preserved for you.

This book was the longest chapter of a larger unpublished manuscript. When I was serving Focus on the Family as their Representative to the United Nations (2001-2010, 2011), I showed the manuscript to my boss, Tom Minnery, then Senior Vice President of Government and Public Policy. He was surprised by the extraordinary passion and influence of the clergy, and recommended that I publish the chapter on the preachers as a stand-alone book with the title, "Fire at the Founding." This is that book!

Because of the great turmoil and division within the United States, now seems the right time to publish it. May it be a useful tool for clergy and Christians in every sphere to empower them to take up their mantels and restore the true and righteous foundations of our nation, and give hope for the future of the United States. May this book also be a great encouragement and inspiration to clergy and Christians in other nations.

Thomas W. Jacobson

2 July 2020 (244th anniversary of vote approving the *Declaration*)
3 April 2024 (revised for 2nd edition)

# FOREWORD

Dr. D. James Kennedy (1930-2007) wrote the forward for the larger manuscript from which the text for the FIRE AT THE FOUNDING was extracted. That larger unpublished manuscript is titled, *Will American Remain Free? The Connection Between True Religion and Liberty Discovered by our Founding Fathers*. Soon after the original work was completed in 1994, the author, Thomas Jacobson, met Dr. D. James Kennedy and gave him a copy of the manuscript, asking if he would write the forward for the book. Dr. Kennedy graciously reviewed the work and wrote the following Forward. Only the parts appropriate to this shorter publication are excerpted from his letter.

> Thomas W. Jacobson . . . has inventoried, perhaps for the first time, the foundational propositions which form the historical connections between true religion and the principles of genuine liberty as enunciated by the Founding Fathers.
>
> In workmanlike fashion, the author . . . reveals . . . both the public perception and moral standards which are irrefutably related to those twin bases [religion and liberty] on which our government was originally established.
>
> The book brings together an exhaustive compilation of significant statements from . . . the champions of religious liberty, the representatives of the clergy . . . .
>
> The importance of this impressive work is found, not just in the preponderance of evidence it amasses, but in the convincing manner by which it confronts the

reader with a demand for making a personal choice. "Will America Remain Free?" The author makes it plain and unequivocal: the answer to that question is up to concerned Americans.

24 May 1994

Dr. James Kennedy, Ph.D.
Senior Minister
Coral Ridge Presbyterian Church

# CHAPTER ONE

# The Fire: The Proper Influence of Clergy

L IBERTY FOR COMMON PEOPLE WAS RARE THROUGHOUT history until Christians understood, based on careful study of Scripture, that God created all men free and accountable to Him, and defined and limited the purpose and powers of civil and religious authorities. A change began in 1215 A.D., when bishops and barons in Great Britain worked together to end injustice and tyrannical rule. They pressured King John to sign the Magna Carta, which limited the king's powers, distributed some government powers among the bishops and barons, and guaranteed some rights and liberties. Even so, for centuries thereafter, church leaders and Christians were persecuted, imprisoned, and burned at the stake. For those who opposed the arbitrary rule of king or state church, their personal property, homes, and churches were sometimes confiscated or destroyed.

## Righteous Liberating Influence: Clergy & Church

The Church, led by the clergy, persevered for centuries in efforts to secure religious and civil liberty to every person, not just the elite, through righteous and peaceful struggle. Through careful Bible study, John Calvin (1509-64), John Knox (1505-72), Martin Luther (1483-1546), and other clergy developed well-reasoned theories about the purpose and limits of civil and religious authority. Building upon their understanding that every person is created "in the image of

God" (Genesis 1:27)[1] – and thus has inherent and equal worth, and is first and foremost accountable to Him – came the recognition of religious and civil liberties given by God to every person. To secure these liberties required self-government and civil government. Self-government was understood to mean properly governing oneself under the authority of God according to His will, and according to the dictates of conscience and the Law of God written on every person's heart, without the necessity or interference of civil or other authorities (Genesis 2:15-17; 3:1-19; Psalm 40:8; Jeremiah 31:33; Romans 2:1-16; Hebrews 8:10; 10:16). The purpose, identity, and authority of civil government will be discussed in later chapters.

Clergy and Christian leaders understood that to protect the religious and civil liberties of every person (including clergy) from abuses of power required the limiting of civil government and state church powers. These revelations led to the Reformation that transformed Europe, the migration of settlers to the American Colonies to create Christian societies, and culminated in the American Revolution.

In the American Colonies, pastors, priests, and Christian leaders were the vanguard of efforts to secure liberty and free forms of government based on the Biblical model of ancient Israel. They had the greatest impact on the minds of present and future generations, both leaders and laity. Apart from their courage and influence, the colonists would not have taken the necessary peaceful, and then self-defense, measures to secure liberty for all Americans. Nor would they have had the wisdom to know how to establish new systems of free government based on self-government and the consent of the people governed, with defined and limited powers. During the last quarter of the 1700s, the Americans won their independence, wrote and ratified State constitutions and the *United States Constitution*, and added the Bill of Rights, all protecting religious and civil liberties.

---

[1] Scripture quotations are from the New American Standard Bible.

Clergymen were the best educated men in the American Colonies. At their core, they were Biblical scholars, teaching doctrines of the Christian faith and morality. But they usually had the best libraries in the community, and their knowledge extended to history, cultures, and even law. Through their pulpits and writings, or itinerant preaching throughout the colonies, they taught what the Bible said about any area of concern, thus igniting the hearts and minds of the people with the knowledge of the truth. Through them, the Spirit of God set ablaze an unquenchable FIRE for Truth, liberty, Godly societies, and limited and lawful government, from New England to Georgia.

As you read excerpts from their sermons and writings, you will see their passionate defense of Truth and righteousness. Their great influence will become clear if you recognize that ideas they espoused became the foundations of our society and systems of government. They taught the people weekly through their sermons, enabled them to view both private and public matters from a Scriptural and historical basis, and also delivered instructive election-day sermons to officials and the public. Citizens and civil leaders relied upon ministers to provide them with truths and principles to guide them in personal, family, church, business, and government matters. Pastors taught and equipped colonists to understand and responsibly steward the religious and civil liberties entrusted to them by the Creator, and the proper purpose of civil government in preserving those liberties.

This noble influence of clergy and Christian leaders began in the American Colonies at the first landing in Virginia in 1607, when one pastor, Rev. John Hunt, planted a cross and dedicated the land to Jesus Christ and the propagation of the Gospel to the whole world. It grew with unprecedented commitment and fervency through the Pilgrims who landed at Plymouth on 11 November 1620. Before disembarking the ship, the Pilgrims wrote and signed the *Mayflower Compact*, binding themselves together by civil covenant:

> In the name of God, Amen. We, whose names are underwritten . . . Having undertaken for the Glory

of God, and the Advancement of the Christian
Faith . . . a Voyage to plant the first Colony in the
northern Parts . . . Do by these Presents, solemnly
and mutually, in the Presence of God and one
another, covenant and combine ourselves together
into a civil Body Politick, for our better Ordering
and Preservation . . . And by Virtue hereof do enact,
constitute, and frame, such just and equal Laws,
Ordinances, Acts, Constitutions, and Officers . . .
for the Good of the Colony; unto which we promise
all due Submission and Obedience.[2]

Their purpose was clear. Their sacrifices were great (half of
them died during the first winter). Their clergy and Christian leaders
gave them a vision for what they could accomplish by creating a new
Christian civilization. But it required binding themselves together by
civil covenant into one Body and forming a civil government for their
"better Ordering and Preservation."

During the 1600s and 1700s, most of the people in the American
Colonies viewed their pastors, and elected Christian government
officials, as important leaders, as fathers, of their communities. Rev.
Calvin Colton (1789-1857), in a *History and Character of American
Revivals of Religion*, said,

(T)he primitive communities of New England were
strictly and properly religious societies, the members
of which had emigrated for conscience sake . . . By the
original terms of association, the public authorities,
civil and ecclesiastic, assumed (whether wisely or
unwisely) a parental guardianship over the morals
and religion of individuals—a guardianship rarely

---

[2] "Mayflower Compact," <u>Sources of Our Liberties: Documentary Origins
of Individual Liberties in the United States Constitution and Bill of Rights</u>,
Richard L. Perry, ed. (Chicago: American Bar Association, 1978), p. 60.

refused for ages ... (F)or more than a century after the first landing of our fathers at Plymouth, religion and the church were sustained by a great uniformity of course.[3]

The paternal influence of Christian leaders, both church and civil, was critical during the founding era. However, after a century, when the communities were established and began to wean themselves from this dependence, the people became complacent. At this time, Rev. Samuel Wigglesworth (1688-1768) and other ministers became deeply concerned about the spiritual condition of the people. In 1733, Wigglesworth delivered a sermon in Boston titled, *An Essay for Reviving Religion*, in which he said,

It is a Truth, that we have a *goodly exterior Form of Religion*; Our *Doctrine, Worship* and *Sacraments* are *Orthodox, Scriptural* and *Divine*. There is external Honour paid to the *Sabbath* [but] ...

The *Powerful Love of the World, and Exorbitant Reach After Riches,* which is become the reigning Temper in Persons of all Ranks in our Land, is alone enough to awaken our concern for abandon'd, slighted and forgotten Religion.[4]

---

[3] Calvin Colton, <u>History and Character of American Revivals of Religion</u> (London: Frederick Westley and A.H. Davis, 1832). Reprinted in the U.S. (New York: AMS Press, Inc., 1973), pp. 44-64. [Virginia Theological Seminary Library (VTS): BV 3773 .C725]

[4] Samuel Wigglesworth, "An Essay for Reviving Religion. A Sermon Delivered at Boston, May 30, 1733" (Boston: S. Kneeland for D. Henchman, 1733), pp. 22-26, 30-31. Reprinted in <u>The Great Awakening: Event and Exegesis</u>, edited by Darrett B. Rutman, The University of New Hampshire (New York: John Wiley & Sons, 1970), pp. 15-18.

## Clergy Taught & Prepared the People & Leaders

One of the effects of the spiritual revivals that occurred during the 1700s was that ministers preached more on public matters, including those beyond the immediate concerns of their congregations and communities. Clergymen reasoned from the Scriptures, the writings of philosophers like John Locke (1632-1704), historical evidence, and a basic understanding of the Laws of God, the laws of nature, and human laws. In so doing, they provided answers to questions about religion, liberty, education, business, public policy, choosing public officials, government, the sovereignty of God over nations, etc. They did not stifle the increased interest in human reason, but demonstrated with power the proper use of human reason, aided by the Holy Spirit, in coming to knowledge of the truth. Thus began a flood of sermons on public matters that did not decrease until the early 1800s. Every chapter of this book is largely built around excerpts from such sermons.

Rev. Jonathan Mayhew, D.D. (1720-1766) of Boston delivered a sermon in 1750, titled, *A Discourse Concerning Unlimited Submission and Non-Resistance to the Higher Powers.* Remember this was 25 years before the War for Independence began. In his preface to the published edition, Dr. Mayhew wrote on the appropriateness of preaching on political and governmental matters.

It is hoped that but few will think the subject of it an improper one to be discoursed on in the pulpit, under a notion that this is *preaching politics*, instead of Christ. However, to remove all prejudices of this sort, I beg it may be remembered that "all Scripture is profitable for doctrine, for reproof, for correction, for instruction in righteousness" (2 Timothy 3:16). Why, then, should not those parts of Scripture which relate to *civil government* be examined and explained from the desk, as well as others? Obedience to the civil magistrate is a Christian duty; and if so, why should not the nature, grounds, and extent of it be considered in a Christian assembly? Besides, if it be said that it is out of character for a Christian minister to meddle with such a subject, this censure will at last fall upon the holy apostles. They write upon it in their epistles to Christian churches; and surely it cannot be deemed either criminal or impertinent to attempt an explanation of their doctrine.[5]

A quarter century later, in 1776, only five weeks before members of the Continental Congress signed the *Declaration of Independence*,

---

[5] Jonathan Mayhew, A.M., D.D., pastor of the West Church in Boston, "A Discourse Concerning Unlimited Submission and Non-Resistance to the Higher Powers: with some Reflections on the Resistance made to King Charles I, and on the Anniversary of his Death: In which the Mysterious Doctrine of that Prince's Saintship and Martyrdom is Unriddled. Delivered in a Sermon preached in the West Meeting-House in Boston the LORD'S-DAY after the 30th of January 1750," (Boston: printed and sold by D. Fowler in Queen-street; and by D. Gookin over against the South Meeting-House, 1750). Reprinted in The Pulpit of the American Revolution. Or, The Political Sermons of the Period of 1776, with a Historical Introduction, Notes, and Illustrations, compiled and edited by John Wingate Thornton, A.M. (New York: Burt Franklin, 1860, reprinted in 1970), pp. 47-48; full sermon: pp. 39-104. [Library of Congress (LOC): 77-114833]

Rev. Samuel West (1730-1807) preached a sermon to public officials of Massachusetts. He concluded with the following exhortation to his fellow gospel ministers, some of whom must have been present.

> (I)t is part of the work and business of a gospel minister to teach his hearers the duty they owe to magistrates. Let us, then, endeavor to explain the nature of their duty faithfully, and show them the difference between liberty and licentiousness; and, while we are animating them to oppose tyranny and arbitrary power, let us inculcate upon them the duty of yielding due obedience to lawful authority. In order to the right and faithful discharge of this part of our ministry, it is necessary that we should thoroughly study the law of nature, the rights of mankind, and the reciprocal duties of governors and governed. By this means we shall be able to guard them against the extremes of slavish submission to tyrants on one hand, and of sedition and licentiousness on the other. We may, I apprehend, attain a thorough acquaintance with the law of nature and the rights of mankind, while we remain ignorant of many technical terms of law.[6]

The clergy did not force the people to conform policies and laws to their understanding of Truth. These learned men explained truths and principles that had direct application to public concerns. The people could study the principles in the Bible and discover evidence

---

[6] Samuel West, A.M., pastor of a Church in Dartmouth, "A Sermon Preached before the Honorable Council, and the Honorable House of Representatives of the Colony of Massachusetts-Bay in New-England." May 29th, 1776. Being the Anniversary for the Election of the Honorable COUNCIL for the Colony. Reprinted in op. cit., Pulpit of the American Revolution, pp. 320-321; full sermon: pp. 259-322.

of the same throughout history, and reach their own conclusions. During those early generations, Americans obviously did conclude that what their clergy taught them was true. Indeed, it was a sovereign work of God through the preaching and teaching by clergymen and spiritual revivals that prepared the way for the lawful and just American Revolution.

## Epilogue on the Influence of Clergy & Christian Leaders, True Religion & Morality

During the past two centuries, most clergy gradually withdrew from preaching and speaking on public and government matters. Their influence and that of the Church within the United States has dwindled to a flickering light. The 1954 Johnson Amendment to the federal tax code, enforced by the Internal Revenue Service, had a chilling effect on clergy and churches by threating withdrawal of tax-exempt status.[7] That policy contradicts the First Amendment to the *U.S. Constitution*. But clergy had already largely withdrawn from providing their noble and wise influence on public matters.

Even so, the LORD has graciously raised up pastors like the late Rev. D. James Kennedy, Ph.D. (1930-2007), of Coral Ridge Presbyterian Church in Fort Lauderdale, Florida. Though a small man in stature, his noble Christian character and courage were just like the mighty preachers of the 1700s. With wisdom, grace, and truth, he boldly addressed countless issues facing our nation. The late Dr. Francis A. Schaeffer (1912-1984) was one of the greatest thinkers, philosophers, historians, and clergymen of the last two centuries. His teachings and books continue to impact many around the world. He taught me to think, that truth was knowable, and to discern truth from error, while studying under him at L'Abri in Switzerland (1982-83). May Almighty God raise up many preachers and lay Christians like them.

---

[7] Pulpit Freedom Sunday: "Public Freedom Sunday FAQ," Alliance Defending Freedom. See: www.speakupmovement.org/church/learnmore/details/5255

In 2008, Alliance Defending Freedom launched the Pulpit Freedom Initiative to "restore the right of each pastor to speak scriptural Truth from the pulpit about moral, social, and governmental issues . . . without fear of losing his church's tax-exempt status."[8] In October 2008, on the first annual Pulpit Freedom Sunday, there were 33 pastors who participated, but since then there have been as many as 1,600. Their sermons would have been viewed as normal during our founding era, but are designed to teach Truth to their congregations and challenge the unconstitutionality of the IRS policy.

In September 2012, Rev. Bill Cook founded America's Black Robe Regiment at Patrick Henry College in Purcellville, Virginia, as an association of patriot pastors endeavoring to secure the Blessings of Liberty to our own and succeeding generations of Americans. Rev. Cook explained: "The organization seeks to establish chapters comprised of two or more pastors in every state and political jurisdiction in America, who will assert their own and the vital leadership and influence of their flocks in state and local government. Members draw inspiration from the clergy of the 1700s who preached the political worldview embodied in our Nation's Founding Charters." Rev. Cook continued:

> The principles found in the Declaration of Independence reflect sermon topics that were preached during the decades leading up to the American Revolution. The Preamble to the Constitution of the United States may have lost its luster in our day, but thanks to the American Pulpit, endured for two-and-a-half centuries as the primary mission of healthy government. Pastors led the way in preaching the political worldview that gave birth to the freest, most prosperous, most generous, most prolific missionary-sending Christian republic in human history. We are calling pastors everywhere to embrace their legacy and

---

[8] Ibid.

champion liberty for current and future generations of Americans (https://brrusa.org).

May this small book be an inspiration to pastors and many more to boldly proclaim the Truth.

Liberty cannot be maintained apart from true religion and morality – true religion being the Judeo-Christian faith in the one true Living God. In his 1796 Farewell Address, President George Washington (1732-1799) expressed understanding of this sober reality when he cautioned the nation:

> Of all the dispositions and habits which lead to political prosperity, religion and morality are indispensable supports. In vain would that man claim the tribute of patriotism who should labor to subvert these great pillars of human happiness—these firmest props of the duties of men and citizens. The mere politician, equally with the pious man, ought to respect and to cherish them. A volume could not trace all their connections with private and public felicity. Let it simply be asked, Where is the security for property, for reputation, for life, if the sense of religious obligation desert the oaths which are the instruments of investigation in courts of justice? And let us with caution indulge the supposition that morality can be maintained without religion. Whatever may be conceded to the influence of refined education on minds of peculiar structure, reason and experience both forbid us to expect that national morality can prevail in exclusion of religious principle (p. 212).[9]

---

[9] George Washington, President of the United States, "Farewell Address, September 17, 1796." A Compilation of the Messages and Papers of the Presidents, by James D. Richardson (Washington: Bureau of National Literature and Art, 1910), George Washington, 1:205-216.

Our own national history and the present tearing apart of our nation internally reveal that, because of our fallen nature, true religion, morality, and liberty cannot be preserved without free, righteous, and courageous clergy and Christians. Any attacks upon them, morality, and the Judeo-Christian faith diminish and ultimately destroy the foundations necessary for both religious and civil liberty for all Americans. The restoration of the pulpit and influence of the Church and Christians, especially noble men, is the only basis of hope for restoring our beloved nation.

## BIBLE STUDY:

1.  What is the Bible? (see 1 Chronicles 17:3; Acts 6:7; 2 Timothy 3:16)

    ......................................................................................................................

2.  Who did the LORD choose to be the priests during the Old Covenant (Exodus 28:1; 29:1)?

    ......................................................................................................................

3.  Who did the LORD give charge of the Law of God and Scriptures (Deuteronomy 31:24-26; Hebrews 7:11)?

    ......................................................................................................................

4.  Who taught the people the Law of God and the Word of God (Exodus 24:7; Leviticus 10:8-11; Numbers 31:21; Nehemiah 8:1-8, 18; 9:3-5; 2 Chronicles 15:3; 17:7-9; Hosea 4:6)?

    ......................................................................................................................

5.  Who else read or was to hear the Law of God and Word of God (Joshua 1:8; 8:30-35; 23:6; 2 Kings 22:8-13; 2 Chronicles 17:7-9)?

    ......................................................................................................................

6.  Who is Jesus (John 1:1; 14:6; 18:37; Ephesians 4:21)?

    ......................................................................................................................

7. Who did Jesus command to abide in, speak and teach His Word (Matthew 10:1-20; 28:18-20; Mark 16:14-20; Luke 24:44-49; John 8:31-32; Acts 1:8)?

   ........................................................................................................

8. Who is the Holy Spirit (John 14:16-17; 15:26-27; 16:13; 1 John 5:6)?

   ........................................................................................................

9. What is the Church (1 Timothy 3:15)?

   ........................................................................................................

10. Were the apostles bold in declaring the Word of God and Truth (Acts 2:14-41; 3:11-26; 4:1-31; 5:17-32)?

   ........................................................................................................

## QUESTIONS FOR CONTEMPLATION OR DISCUSSION:

1. Who brought clarity about religious and civil liberty, and the limits of church and civil government authorities, from the 1500s through the 1700s?

   ........................................................................................................

2. What is self-government?

   ........................................................................................................

3. Who were the most well-educated and influential men in the American Colonies?

   ........................................................................................................

4. Who taught the Americans the principles of liberty and civil government?

   ........................................................................................................

5. What other types of leaders were influential in guiding the New England colonists in establishing righteous and just societies?

   ........................................................................................................

6. Do pastors and priests have the duty to teach the truth about liberty, religious freedom, morality, social matters, public policy and government?

..................................................................................................................

7. What is the difference between liberty and licentiousness?

..................................................................................................................

8. Can liberty be maintained or restored apart from true religion and morality?

..................................................................................................................

## SERMON OUTLINE SUGGESTION:

1. Does the Bible address moral, social, public, government and national matters?
2. Who spoke in the Bible about such matters (in the Old Testament; Jesus; apostles)?
3. Who taught Americans about such matters during the 1600s and 1700s?
4. Should pastors today speak on such matters?

# CHAPTER TWO

# Public Recognition of the Sovereignty of Almighty God & Keeping The Sabbath & Lord's Day Holy

UNTIL RECENT DECADES, AMERICANS BELIEVED IT WAS right and appropriate to give public recognition to Almighty God. The preachers, private leaders, public officials, and legislators, including those who wrote colonial and state charters and constitutions as well as the Declaration of Independence (our national charter that formed the United States of America), were careful to acknowledge God and His sovereignty by mentioning Him by name. They also indirectly acknowledged Him by stating principles of religion, liberty, and government from or consistent with the Scriptures; and by conforming most aspects of the constitutions and laws to the Law of God. By doing so, they ensured equal protection of God-given inalienable liberties of the people, and civil governments that, at least by design, did not exceed their legitimate bounds.

Dr. Jonathan Mayhew, in his 1750 sermon on Romans 13, titled, a *Discourse Concerning Unlimited Submission and Non-Resistance to the Higher Powers,* observed the following about the character of God, the Creator and Ruler of all nations:

> . . . God Himself does not govern in an absolutely arbitrary and despotic manner . . . the power of this almighty King is limited by law; not indeed by acts of

Parliament, but by the eternal laws of truth, wisdom, and equity, and the everlasting tables of right reason.[10]

Rev. Gad Hitchcock (1719-1803) gave an *Election Sermon* in 1774. Speaking to the people of Boston, Massachusetts, he said, "we cannot forbear the acclamation of the psalmist … happy is that people whose God is the LORD!"[11]

Dr. Samuel Langdon (1723-1797) preached before the Congress of the Massachusetts-Bay Colony in 1775, about the sovereignty of God in relation to human governments.

We must keep our eyes fixed on the supreme government of the Eternal King, as directing all events, setting up or pulling down the kings of the earth at His pleasure, suffering the best forms of human government to degenerate and go to ruin by

---

[10] Op. cit., Jonathan Mayhew, "Unlimited Submission," p. 95.

[11] Gad Hitchcock, pastor of Congregational Church, Pembroke, Massachusetts, "An Election Sermon" (Boston, 1774). Reprinted in <u>American Political Writing During the Founding Era, 1760-1805</u>, 2 Volumes, written, compiled and edited by Charles S. Hyneman and Donald S. Lutz (Indianapolis: Liberty Press, 1983), 1:296-297, 302.

corruption, or restoring the decayed constitutions of kingdoms and states by reviving public virtue and religion, and granting the favorable interpositions of His providence.[12]

Rev. Samuel West delivered an election day sermon on May 29, 1776, before the government of Massachusetts. To these officials, he declared,

> Unlimited submission and obedience is due to none but God alone. He has an absolute right to command; He alone has an uncontrollable sovereignty over us, because He alone is unchangeably good.[13]

Rev. Timothy Stone (1742-1797), pastor of the Congregationalist Church of Lebanon, Connecticut, delivered *An Election Sermon* in 1792. He observed the sovereignty of Jesus Christ over human affairs, and the blessings or judgments that He renders to nations.

> That religion, which GOD hath enjoined upon rational beings, is not only necessary for His glory, but essential to their happiness. To establish a character as being truly religious, under the light of divine revelation, it is by no means sufficient, that men should barely acknowledge the existence, and general providence of one supreme DEITY. From this heavenly light, we obtain decided evidence, that

---

[12] Samuel Langdon, D.D., "Government Corrupted by Vice, and Recovered by Righteousness. A sermon preached before the Honorable Congress of the Colony of the Massachusetts-Bay" on Wednesday the 31st day of May 1775. Reprinted in op. cit., Pulpit of the American Revolution, p. 238; full sermon: pp. 227-258.

[13] Op. cit., Samuel West, "A Sermon Preached before the Honorable Council, and the Honorable House of Representatives," p. 283.

the Almighty Father, hath set His well beloved Son the blessed IMMANUEL, as King upon His holy hill of Zion. This DIVINE person, in His mediatorial character, "is exalted, far above all principality, and power, and might, and dominion, and every name that is named, not only in this world, but also, in that which is to come. And all things are put under His feet. That at the name of JESUS, every knee should bow, of things in heaven, and things in earth, and things under the earth; and that every tongue should confess, that JESUS CHRIST is LORD, to the glory of GOD the Father" [Romans 4:11; Ephesians 1:19-23; Philippians 2:9-11] . . .

Communities, have their existence in, and from, this glorious personage. The kingdom is His, and He ruleth among the nations. Through His bounty, and special providence, it is, that a people enjoy the inestimable liberties and numerous advantages of a well-regulated civil society: through His influence, they are inspired with understanding to adopt, with strength and public spirit to maintain, a righteous constitution: He gives able impartial rulers, to guide in paths of virtue and peace; or gets up over them the basest of men. By His invisible hand, states are preserved from internal convulsions, and shielded by His Almighty arm from external violence: or, through His providential displeasure, they are given as a prey to their own vices; or to the lusts and passions of other states, to be destroyed.[14]

---

[14] Timothy Stone, pastor of Congregationalist Church of Lebanon, Connecticut, "An Election Sermon" (Hartford, 1792). Reprinted in op. cit., American Political Writing, 2:849-852.

Americans enjoyed "the inestimable liberties and numerous advantages of a well-regulated civil society" after they won the War for Independence and ratified the *United States Constitution*. For generations, Americans also enjoyed many "able impartial rulers" who guided us "in paths of virtue and peace." However, as we enjoyed these blessings from God in the past, we are now experiencing His judgments since we have rejected Him. Rev. Stone continued with this caution,

> Thus absolutely dependent, are temporal communities, and all human things, upon HIM who reigneth King in Zion. "Be wise now therefore, O ye kings; be instructed, ye judges of the earth. Kiss the Son lest He be angry, and ye perish from the way, when His wrath is kindled but a little: blessed are all they that put their trust in Him."[15] [Psalm 2:10-12]

## Keeping The Sabbath Day or The Lord's Day Holy

When I was a child, most Americans were still faithfully keeping Sunday as the LORD's Day or Saturday as the Sabbath Day, as a day to worship God personally and corporately, rest, and be with their families. This was in obedience to the Fourth Commandment (Exodus 20:8-11), which was based on God's order in Creation (Genesis 2:2-3). For believers in Jesus Christ as the Messiah, on the day of His resurrection, this changed to Sunday, the LORD's Day (Matthew 28:1-7; Mark 16:1-14; Luke 24:1-47; John 20:1-20; Acts 20:7; Revelation 1:10). When we keep that Day every week, we reaffirm our dependence upon God, as individuals and as a nation, for His protection, provision, and blessings.

When our Founding Fathers wrote the *United States Constitution*, they fulfilled the Fourth Commandment by not requiring any action

---

[15] Ibid.

on legislation on the LORD's Day. When the president of the United States receives a bill passed by both houses of Congress, he has 10 days to sign or veto it. If, however, the tenth day falls upon a Sunday, he does not need to return it until the following day.[16]

In the 1740s, Rev. Thomas Bacon (1711-1768), minister of the Protestant Episcopal Church in Maryland, spoke about the Sabbath and the LORD's Day. This was in a time when the evil of slavery existed in the United States. His concern was that servants and slaves receive needed rest from their labors in the same way that everyone else had the opportunity to rest. This excerpt is from a collection of his sermons titled, *Sermons Addressed To Masters And Servants.*

The seventh day was set apart as a day of rest and devotion; not only as a memorial of the creation, but to the *Israelites* was also to be a perpetual remembrance of their delivery from the bondage of the *Egyptians*: . . . The LORD's Day, which succeeded to the *Sabbath* of the *Israelites,* is a standing memorial of this our redemption, as well as [of] creation; and

---

[16] United States Constitution, Art. 1, Sec. 7, par. 2.

our servants have an equal title to the benefits of it.... How much more then ought we to labour, that our slaves may partake of the blessings of the Gospel; and thereby be enabled to *enter into* that *everlasting rest of the people of God (Hebrews 4:11), which they have as much right* to as we have?[17]

Rev. Bacon believed that masters had a responsibility before God to *not* require their servants and slaves to work on the LORD's Day.

Rev. Amos Adams (1728-1775), pastor of the First Church in Roxbury, preached on the day called for a General Fast, 6 April 1769. He spoke of the great importance of private and public observance of the LORD's Day.

The serious and conscientious observance of the LORD's-day is a duty of the highest importance to the life and power of religion among a people.... (R)eligion prospers or declines among a people, according to the respect that is shown to the LORD's-day ... So far as the LORD's-day becomes a season for visiting, feasting, gaming and diversions, the life of Christianity will expire, and all manner of vices grow among a people. Only cast your eyes on those places, where little regard is paid to the LORD's-day, and you will find them, in a state of ignorance,

---

[17] Thomas Bacon, Minister of the Protestant Episcopal Church in Maryland, "Sermon 1," <u>Sermons Addressed to Masters and Servants</u>. Republished with other Tracts and Dialogues on the same subject, and recommended to all Masters and Mistresses to be used in their families, by Rev. William Meade (Winchester, VA: John Heiskell, printer, 1813). 238 pages. [Howard University (HU) Library, Moorland-Springarn Collection (MSC): M326 .27 B13]

and immorality, little or nothing better than absolute heathenism.[18]

In recent decades, America has become one of those "places, where little regard is paid to the LORD's-day." Rev. Adams' description, given more than 250 years ago, of what becomes of such nations, is descriptive of the United States today, and other nations. Just as Almighty God relates to individual nations, so also by their beliefs and practices the people of a nation respond to God, revealing whether He is their God. How or whether individuals keep the day holy is a matter of personal discretion, but if the people do not collectively decide to keep the Sabbath or LORD's Day holy, that is the decision they live out before God. I know of no nation in history that was able to preserve reverential fear of God, righteousness, purity, and liberty after they failed to collectively and publicly keep the Sabbath or LORD's Day holy.

I don't believe we will see America restored to her former glory until we as a nation recover our reverence for and confidence in Almighty God, publicly honor Him, restore and protect the symbols that honor Him, and restore voluntary united observance of the LORD's Day, or for Jews, the Sabbath Day.

## BIBLE STUDY:

1. What happened when Moses and Aaron repeatedly honored the LORD God publicly and spoke representing Him to

---

[18] Amos Adams, A.M., Pastor of the First Church in Roxbury, "A concise, historical view of the perils, hardships, difficulties and discouragements which have attended the planting and progressive improvements of *New-England*; with a particular account of its long and destructive wars, expensive expeditions, &c. With reflections, *principally*, moral and religious. In Two Discourses, Preached at Roxbury on the General Fast, April 6, 1769" (Boston: printed and sold by Kneeland and Adams, 1769), p. 54; 66 pages. [LOC: F7 .A2 Office]

Pharoah and Egypt, to let God's people go from bondage (Exodus 5:1-2; 6:1-9; 7:1-22; 8:10, 19-23; etc.)?

.........................................................................................................

2. What happened when young David spoke boldly on the battlefield for the LORD against Goliath who was taunting God's people Israel (1 Samuel 17)?

.........................................................................................................

3. What happened when Daniel and his three friends publicly held fast to the LORD, and spoke boldly to King Nebuchadnezzar and the Babylonians (Daniel 3:1-4:37)?

.........................................................................................................

4. When did the LORD establish the Sabbath Day (Genesis 2:2-3; Exodus 16:22-30; 20:8-11)?

.........................................................................................................

5. Why was ancient Israel taken into captivity by Babylon for exactly 70 years (2 Chronicles 36:20-21; Jeremiah 25:8-11; Daniel 9:2)?

.........................................................................................................

6. When did Sunday become the LORD's Day (Matthew 28:1-7; Mark 16:1-14; Luke 24:1-47; John 20:1-20; Acts 20:7; Revelation 1:10)?

.........................................................................................................

7. Who are the happiest and most blessed people on earth (Psalm 33:12; 144:15)?

.........................................................................................................

8. Who is Jesus described as in Ephesians 1:20-23?

.........................................................................................................

9. What are the first steps of decline for a person or nation (Romans 1:18-21)?

.........................................................................................................

23

## QUESTIONS FOR CONTEMPLATION OR DISCUSSION:

1. Compare public recognition of the LORD during the founding generations to public recognition of the LORD today in the United States (or your nation)?

   .............................................................................................................

2. Compare the founding generations acknowledgement of the LORD's Day or Sabbath Day to observation of it today in the United States (or your nation)?

   .............................................................................................................

3. What provision in the United States Constitution honors the LORD's Day?

   .............................................................................................................

4. Why did Rev. West say that "unlimited submission" and obedience is "due to God alone"?

   .............................................................................................................

5. Through Whom can a "people enjoy the inestimable liberties and numerous advantages of a well-regulated civil society"?

   .............................................................................................................

6. Why is it important for an individual to keep the LORD's Day or Sabbath Day holy to the LORD each week?

   .............................................................................................................

7. What is a principal cause of "the life of Christianity" decreasing and expiring, and ignorance, immorality, and heathenism increasing, in a nation?

   .............................................................................................................

8. What are some practical steps that we as Christians can take to reestablish the Sabbath (Saturday or Sunday) as a day of worship and rest in our own lives?

   .............................................................................................................

9. What are some practical steps that we as Christians can take to reestablish the Sabbath in our communities, educational systems, and local and state governments?

.................................................................................................................

## SERMON OUTLINE SUGGESTION:

1. What are the benefits of personally acknowledging God in public, versus the effects of not doing so?
2. What are the benefits of a community or nation acknowledging God publicly, versus the consequences of not doing so?
3. What are the benefits of keeping the LORD's Day or Sabbath Day holy, versus the consequences of not doing so?

## CHAPTER THREE

# Liberty Recognized as a Gift from God & Virtue Necessary to Preserve

THE PILGRIMS AND PURITANS WHO SETTLED NEW ENGLAND in the 1600s, the Founding Fathers during the 1700s, and most Americans until recent generations, recognized liberty as an unalienable gift from God the Creator. They founded the American Colonies and later the United States primarily to gain and preserve religious and civil liberty.

Rev. Levi Hart (1738-1808), pastor of the Congregational Church in Preston, Connecticut, gave a sermon in 1775 titled, *Liberty Described and Recommended*. He explained several types of liberty and bondage.

> Religious liberty is the opportunity of professing and practicing *that religion* which is agreeable to our judgment and consciences, without interruption or punishment from the civil magistrate. And religious bondage or slavery, is when we may not do this without incurring the penalty of laws, and being exposed to suffer in our persons or property.
>
> Ecclesiastical liberty, is such a state of order and regularity in Christian society, as gives every member opportunity to fill up his place in acting for the general good of that great and holy society to which the true church of Christ belongs, and of which they are a part....

Spiritual liberty then, is freedom or readiness and engagedness of soul in the love and service of God and Christ, and discharge of the various branches of Christian duty.

Spiritual bondage, takes place in the dominion of sin and Satan in the soul, or that state of alienation from God and Christ, to which all impenitent sinners are subject.[19]

Rev. Jacob Duché (1738-1798) was the Episcopalian minister who opened the Continental Congress of 1774 with prayer, and was selected in 1776 as its chaplain. On 7 July 1775, he preached a sermon at Christ Church of Philadelphia, titled, *The Duty Of Standing Fast In Our Liberties*. He dedicated it to General Washington, recently appointed Commander-In-Chief of the Continental Army.

"Stand fast, therefore, in the liberty wherewith Christ hath made us free" (Galatians 5:1)....

---

[19] Levi Hart, pastor of Congregational Church, Preston, Connecticut, "Liberty Described and Recommended: A Sermon Preached to the Corporation of Freemen in Farmington" (Hartford, 1775). Reprinted in op. cit., <u>American Political Writing</u>, 1:311.

> And I believe it will be no difficult matter to prove
> that (civil liberty) is as much the gift of God in Christ
> Jesus as (spiritual liberty), and consequently, that
> we are bound to stand fast in our civil as well as our
> spiritual freedom.

> ... (L)iberty, traced to her true source, is of heavenly
> extraction, that divine virtue is her illustrious parent,
> that from eternity to eternity they have been and
> must be inseparable companions ... that when man
> lost his virtue, he lost his liberty too.[20]

Rev. Duché recognized virtue and liberty as "inseparable companions" that were gifts of God. Is it not true that as America has lost its virtue it is losing its liberties too?

Rev. Elisha Rich (1740-1812), pastor of the Church of Christ in Chelmsford, Massachusetts, preached *A Sermon On Ecclesiastical Liberty* in 1775. He made an important distinction between liberty from spiritual bondage and the religious liberty that is a right of every person.

> 1 Corinthians 7:23
> "Ye are bought with a price; be not ye the servants
> of men:" ...

> There is indeed, two different kinds of liberty
> contained in the text, first, Liberty from spiritual
> bondage, viz. from the power of sin. Secondly,
> Liberty from worldly mastership in religion, the

---

[20] Jacob Duché, "The Duty Of Standing Fast In Our Liberties. A Sermon preached in Christ Church, in Philadelphia," on July 7, 1775, and dedicated to General Washington. Reprinted in The Patriot Preachers of the American Revolution. With Biographical Sketches. Edited by Frank Moore (New York: Charles T. Evans, 1862), pp. 80-81; full sermon: pp. 74-89. [LOC: E 297 .M682]

first of these none have a right to, but [except] those who are true believers in Christ: But the second, viz. Freedom from worldly mastership in religion, all rational beings have a right to, since all men must give an account to God, for all things that concerns religious principles or practice; so that in religion, none ought to be servants of men. . . .

(A)ll Christ's servants are bought *free*, not only from the power of sin, but all worldly mastership.[21]

On 26 May 1779, during the War for Independence, Dr. Samuel Stillman (1737-1807) preached a sermon before the public officials of the State of Massachusetts Bay, titled, *The Duty of Magistrates*. He delivered it prior to the convention to form a state constitution. Knowing that the officials shared his convictions, he said, "With us, it is a first and fundamental principle, that God made all men equal . . . And as they are equal, so they are likewise in a state of entire freedom."[22]

Rev. Timothy Stone said in an *Election Sermon*, "Through (Jesus Christ's) bounty, and special providence, it is, that a people enjoy the inestimable liberties and numerous advantages of a well-regulated civil society."[23]

---

[21] Elisha Rich, minister of the Gospel, and pastor of a Church of Christ in Chelmsford. "A Sermon on Ecclesiastical Liberty. Preached soon after the Civil War (commenced), Between Great-Britain and the American Colonies. In the Year 1775. In which the free bought Man's Liberty is Vindicated" (Concord, New England: Nathaniel Coverly, for the author, 1776), p. 7. [LOC: BV 741 .R5 Rare Book Collection]

[22] Samuel Stillman, D.D. "The Duty of Magistrates. A Sermon preached before the Honorable Council and Honorable House of Representatives of the State of Massachusetts Bay," on May 26th, 1779. It was also preached before the Supreme Court of Massachusetts, on May 29, 1779. Reprinted in op. cit., The Patriot Preachers of the American Revolution, p. 264.

[23] Op. cit., Timothy Stone, "An Election Sermon," see pg. 88.

In the 1600s and 1700s, American preachers taught the people that their liberties were from God. The Pilgrims and Puritans knew this to be true even before they immigrated, which is why they fled from oppression to find an asylum for liberty. As they grew in their understanding that their liberties were the gift of God, they realized these were also inalienable rights. *Webster's 1828 Dictionary* defines "inalienable" as something which "cannot be legally or justly alienated or transferred to another."[24] Their liberties were inalienable based on the sovereignty of God. If the Sovereign gave them certain liberties to them, no human authority had the right to take them away. Indeed, a primary purpose of civil government is to protect inalienable rights.

A nation that denies the sovereignty of God has no basis for declaring certain liberties or rights inalienable. Where else would liberty or inalienable human rights come from? A liberty or right given by man or human government is not inalienable, and can always be taken away. If we believe that our government gives us our liberties and rights, then our government can take them away at will. However, our Founding Fathers believed that inalienable liberties and rights are from the Creator (see *Declaration of Independence*, paragraphs 1-2). They identified the liberties and rights God had given to all men, and created forms of government with constitutional provisions to protect and preserve them. Americans did not fight the War for Independence to gain liberties or rights from the English government. Once they had declared independence and won the war, they were no longer under England's power. Their liberty was not from England, though they were free from her oppression.

Another consequence of denying the sovereignty of God is the loss of virtue, which results in the loss of liberty. *Webster's 1828 Dictionary* defined "virtue" as:

---

[24] Noah Webster, <u>An American Dictionary of the English Language</u>, 1828 ed. (New York: published by S. Converse; printed by Hezekiah Howe of New Haven). Reprinted by The Foundation for American Christian Education, San Francisco, CA (New York: The Iversen-Norman Associates, 1967, 1980, 1983), s.v. "inalienable."

1. Strength; 2. Bravery; valor; 3. Moral goodness;
the practice of moral duties and the abstaining from
vice . . . a conformity of life and conversation to the
moral law . . . The practice of moral duties merely
from motives of convenience, or from compulsion,
or from regard to reputation, is *virtue*, as distinct from
*religion*. The practice of moral duties from sincere love
to God and His laws, is virtue and religion . . . *Virtue*
is nothing but voluntary obedience to truth. *Dwight*.[25]

If a people are virtuous, loving and respect one another and
voluntarily uphold God's moral law, then they can be spiritually free
(internal) and are capable of preserving civil liberty (external). If
their desire to be virtuous is motivated by love for God, and they
instill true religion and virtue in their children, then virtue and liberty
can be preserved from one generation to another. Those who do not
love God can demonstrate virtue by doing what is right, regardless of
their motives. However, if they reject the moral law of God, what will
motivate them to do what is right? What will keep them from doing
evil? Ultimately, fear alone will motivate those who have rejected
God's love and His moral law. Consequently, if a nation rejects "the
moral law" of God, it will lose its virtue. If it loses its virtue, it will lack
the discipline to be self-governing and be unable to sustain religious
and civil liberty, as well as a free, just, and limited form of government.

Rev. Duché said that "divine virtue is (liberty's) illustrious
parent, [and] that from eternity to eternity they have been and must
be inseparable companions." In other words, if people will voluntarily
govern themselves according to the moral law of God written in
Scripture and on their hearts, they can be free. God Almighty makes
the rules. If we don't abide by them, we won't be free.

**Liberty is the responsible use of freedom**! If people are not
responsible with their liberties, they will lose them. A nation that

---

[25] Ibid., s.v. "virtue."

rejects the sovereignty of God and His good and moral Law, and whose people choose not to be virtuous and responsible, cannot remain a free nation, at least not for very long. Americans today are in grave danger of losing all of the priceless liberties that four centuries of Americans labored, fought and died in order to preserve for us.

Even so there is hope. The United States, like every other nation in history, has faced one or more periods of spiritual and moral decline, though never as low as our current state. Yet if the people of God, responding to the Spirit of God, and wonderfully influenced and inspired by clergy and Christian leaders, humble themselves, repent of and turn from their personal and national sins, returning to God, then they will see the goodness and mercy of God (2 Chronicles 7:12-14). The knowledge of God, righteousness and justice, religious and civil liberty, morality and integrity, and respect for clergy and the Church can all be restored.

## BIBLE STUDY:

1. What type of liberty does Isaiah 61:1 proclaim that "The Spirit of the LORD GOD" brings?

   ............................................................................................................................

2. What is the connection between the Spirit of God and liberty (2 Corinthians 3:17)?

   ............................................................................................................................

3. Describe a person who abides by "the perfect law, the law of liberty," by the power of the Holy Spirit within him (James 1:23-25):

   ............................................................................................................................

4. Read Galatians 5:1, 13-25. What does this Scripture reveal of the connections between Christ, freedom, self-government and virtue evidenced by the fruit of the Holy Spirit?

   ............................................................................................................................

5.  Read 1 Corinthians 7:23. What does this verse say about religious liberty and spiritual liberty (see this chapter's text above and questions below)?

    ......................................................................................................................

6.  Why did GOD make us free, and give us liberty to obey or not obey Him?

    ......................................................................................................................

7.  From Biblical evidence and life experience, do you think people flourish when they have liberty and are self-governing? Why?

    ......................................................................................................................

## QUESTIONS FOR CONTEMPLATION OR DISCUSSION:

1.  What is liberty? The first American Dictionary of the English Language, published by Noah Webster in 1828, defines *Liberty* as "Freedom from restraint . . . to the body . . . will or mind." How does that definition compare with a current definition?

    ......................................................................................................................

2.  Webster's 1828 defines *"Religious liberty" as* "the free right . . . of opinions on religious subjects, and of worshipping the Supreme Being according to the dictates of conscience, without external control." What aspects of Rev. Hart's definition expound this?

    ......................................................................................................................

3.  What is religious bondage?

    ......................................................................................................................

4.  What is civil liberty? Webster's 1828: "*Civil liberty* is the liberty of men in a state of society . . . only abridged and restrained as is necessary and expedient for the safety and interest of

the society, state or nation." How does that compare with a current dictionary?

.........................................................................................................

5.  What types of liberty has God given to all mankind?

.........................................................................................................

6.  What is liberty connected to and necessary to preserve it? What is the "inseparable companion" of liberty?

.........................................................................................................

7.  What is virtue?

.........................................................................................................

8.  Who has a right to religious freedom, to "liberty from worldly mastership in religion"?

.........................................................................................................

9.  Who has a right to "liberty of spiritual bondage," to freedom "from the power of sin"?

.........................................................................................................

10. What are "inalienable rights"?

.........................................................................................................

11. Are liberty and religious freedom inalienable rights given by God?

.........................................................................................................

12. "Liberty is the responsible use of............................................................."

.........................................................................................................

13. What is possible if a people are self-governing, virtuous, loving, and respectful under God?

.........................................................................................................

14. What are consequences of rejecting God, His moral Law, and virtue?

   ............................................................................................................

15. If a nation rejects God and loses its virtue, what must they do to be restored?

   ............................................................................................................

## SERMON OUTLINE SUGGESTIONS:

1. What is liberty?
2. What is virtue?
3. How are they inseparable companions?

<br>

1. What are religious liberty and spiritual liberty?
2. What is civil liberty?
3. Is liberty from God, and if so, how do we cherish, protect, and restore it?

# CHAPTER FOUR

# American Colonies Settled as an Asylum for Liberty & True Religion

P ILGRIMS, PURITANS, SEPARATISTS, PIONEERS, homesteaders and others came from many nations to the American Colonies seeking an asylum for religious and civil liberty because they were persecuted, oppressed and tortured by ecclesiastical and civil authorities for their religious beliefs in their native lands. When the Pilgrims arrived at Cape Cod on 11 November 1620 to establish the Plymouth Settlement, they wrote and signed the Mayflower Compact that declared their purpose:

> In the name of God, Amen. We, whose names are underwritten ... Having undertaken for the Glory of God, and the Advancement of the Christian Faith....[26]

Governor William Bradford, first governor of Plymouth, wrote this about their purpose and history:

> (T)hey cherished a great hope and inward zeal of laying good foundations, or at least of making some way towards it, for the propagation and advance of the gospel of the kingdom of Christ in the remotest parts of the world, even though they should be but

---

[26] Op. cit., "Mayflower Compact."

stepping stones to others in the performance of so great a work.[27]

Generations later, on the day of a General Fast, 6 April 1769, Rev. Amos Adams of Roxbury, Massachusetts, preached on the "perils, hardships, difficulties and discouragements" encountered in "the planting and progressive improvements of *New-England*." He expounded on what Americans in that period considered undeniable facts regarding their settlement of the New England Colonies.

It is a truth, impossible to be denied, that the spiritual tyranny, under which our fathers groaned, and their being inhibited the worship of God, according to the light of their own consciences, was the cause of their leaving their native country, to plant themselves in this howling wilderness. It was this abridgment of the rights of conscience that began and mightily assisted in the settlement of this country. The oppression under which a valuable part of the nation groaned, has, in the hand of Consummate Wisdom, proved, in its consequences, a great blessing to the world . . . as well, as of a glorious enlargement of the kingdom of the Redeemer. The LORD our God hath turned the curse into a blessing. . . .

This country was at first sought and settled as an Asylum for liberty, civil and religious . . . And this is what we may always expect, that a government so popular and friendly to liberty as this, will always be the envy and hatred of the abettors of tyranny, in Great-Britain, as well as among ourselves. . . .

---

[27] William Bradford, <u>Of Plymouth Plantation: 1620-1647</u>. Rendered into Modern English by Harold Paget, 1909, and republished under title, <u>Bradford's History of the Plymouth Settlement</u> (San Antonio, Texas: Mantle Ministries, 1988), p. 21.

The views on which this land was settled were singular and noble: It was not trade and commerce, nor any worldly views, but religion was the noble motive that brought our fathers hither, and reconciled them to the perils of their wilderness state. They planted themselves *here* with the real express views of serving God, and of training up their posterity in the good ways of the LORD.[28]

Rev. Adams and many of the colonists were able to view the oppressions they escaped as blessings because they motivated them to leave "their native country" and come to the wilderness in America. He also observed that the "abettors of tyranny," even in America, who favored government control of the lives of the people were always envious and hateful of a government that carefully protected the liberties of the people.

Rev. William Gordon (1728-1807), pastor of the Third Church in Roxbury, had great influence in the Colonies. On 15 December 1774, a day set aside by the Provincial Congress, he preached at the Boston Lecture, reminding the people of the original reason their ancestors came to America.

(T)he ancestors of this people were eminently godly; it was the strength of their zeal for true,

---

[28] Op. cit., Amos Adams, "A concise, historical view of the perils . . . With reflections, *principally*, moral and religious," pp. 7-8, 51-52, 63-64.

unadulterated religion, and the ardor of their love to God and Christ, that prevailed upon them to venture over the great deep, and to seek an abode in this then inhospitable and dangerous country, and that reconciled them to the numberless difficulties that they had long to encounter without ever attaining to the various comforts that we enjoy. They were concerned to perpetuate the same spirit of piety which they were actuated by; paid great attention to the rising generation, and wisely provided for the good instruction of succeeding ones.[29]

Rev. Samuel West, in his 1776 sermon to Massachusetts-Bay public leaders, said "Providence has designed this continent to be the asylum of liberty and true religion."

Our fathers fled from the rage of prelatical [high church office] tyranny and persecution, and came into this land in order to enjoy liberty of conscience . . . Many have been the interpositions of Divine Providence on our behalf, both in our fathers' days and ours . . . I cannot help hoping, and even believing, that Providence has designed this continent to be the asylum of liberty and true religion; for can we suppose that the God who created us free agents, and designed that we should glorify and serve Him in this world that we might enjoy Him forever hereafter, will suffer liberty and

---

[29] William Gordon, pastor of the Third Church in Roxbury, Massachusetts, "A Discourse Preached on December 15th, 1774, Being the day recommended by the Provincial Congress; and *afterwards* (preached) *at the* Boston LECTURE." Reprinted in op. cit., Pulpit of the American Revolution, pp. 207-208; full sermon: pp. 191-226.

true religion to be banished from off the face of the earth.[30]

What is true religion? Webster's 1828 Dictionary first defines "religion" generally (1) – describing true religion – and then broadly (4) as "any system of faith and worship." Unlike modern dictionaries, it distinguishes "false religion" from "true religion."

1. Religion, in its most comprehensive sense, includes a belief in the being and perfection of God, in the revelation of His will to man, in man's obligation to obey His commands, in a state of reward and punishment, and in man's accountableness to God; and also true godliness or piety of life, with the practice of all moral duties. It therefore comprehends theology, as a system of doctrines or principles, as well as practical piety; for the practice of moral duties without a belief in a divine lawgiver, and without reference to His will or commands, is not religion.
2. Any system of faith and worship. In this sense, religion comprehends the belief and worship of pagans and Mohammedans, as well as of Christians; any religion consisting in the belief of a superior power or powers governing the world, and in the worship of such power or powers. Thus we speak of the religion of the Turks, of the Hindoos, of the Indians, etc., as well as of the Christian religion. We speak of *false religion*, as well as of *true religion*.[31]

In 1794, Rev. Thomas Dunn (1742-1802), spoke before the New York Society for the Information and Assistance of Persons Emigrating from Foreign Countries. He recounted the history of the colonization of America, and stated that the Pilgrims (Separatists)

---

[30] Op. cit., Samuel West, "A Sermon Preached before the Honorable Council, and the Honorable House of Representatives," p. 311.

[31] Op., cit., Noah Webster, <u>An American Dictionary of the English Language</u>, s.v. "religion."

came to America "as the only asylum for liberty and religion left in the world."

> In the year 1606 a congregation of pious Christians, and their Pastor, Mr. Robinson, being extremely harassed and persecuted, for their religious opinions, determined to quit England. They were alarmed by a cruel act, which was to punish Nonconformity, in some cases with perpetual banishment, and in others with death: and they were too conscientious to conform to the Established Episcopal Church, by adopting ceremonies which appeared to them superstitious, unscriptural, and sinful. They, therefore, resolved to elude their persecutors, by a flight to Holland. Not finding there the state of religion altogether agreeable to their wishes, and feeling an increasing dislike to all the old governments of Europe, they turned a wishful eye towards this country, as the only asylum for liberty and religion left in the world.[32]

They came to America to secure an "asylum for liberty and religion." Peter Marshall and David Manuel, in *The Light and the Glory*, discovered a dramatic contrast between the Pilgrims and Puritans who founded Plymouth, Massachusetts, and those who came to Jamestown, Virginia. At Jamestown, almost all who came on the first ship in 1607, and most who followed for two decades, came only for personal gain. They came for gold and riches. On that first ship, there were 144 men, but no women or children. Obviously,

---

[32] Thomas Dunn, "A Discourse, Delivered before the New York Society for the Information and Assistance of Persons Emigrating from Foreign Countries." October 21, 1794. Reprinted in <u>Pamphlets on Religion and Democracy: 16th to 19th Centuries</u>. Work performed by the Temple of Religion and Tower of Peace (San Francisco, CA: Sutto Library Project for the U.S. Works Projects Administration, July 4, 1940), p. 340. [LOC: BV 741 .C27]

they did not plan to build a permanent settlement. They chose an unhealthy, swampy area, and did not plant a crop for 20 years. Those from wealthy families refused to do any labor, and expected the others to labor for them. When they had no provisions left, they survived by stealing from the Indians. At least 90 percent of those who came to Jamestown during those first two decades died an early death.[33] In was at Jamestown, in 1619, that the first slave ship arrived, and slavery was introduced in North America.

In comparison, the Pilgrims came as families to plant a permanent settlement. They arrived at Plymouth in late 1620, at the onset of winter. Half of the 102 died that first winter, due to illness and the harsh weather conditions. When the weather permitted the next spring, with the help of Indian friends, they began to plant crops and build shelters, which greatly reduced their loss of life.

The Pilgrims considered these sacrifices as part of the cost of liberty, not so much for themselves, but for their children and future generations. They had some freedom of religion in Holland, but knew that their religious and civil liberties were still restricted, and the culture surrounding them was corrupt. Therefore, they came to America to find an asylum to preserve religious and civil liberty for their posterity.

Today, should we not make equal efforts and sacrifices to restore America as an asylum, as a refuge, as a safe place on earth, for true religious and civil liberty? But liberty is the gift of God, and can be preserved only in truth, righteousness, morality, virtue, noble self-government and justice. What blocks that restoration? What is robbing us of our liberties? We are a nation full of personal and national sin, full of idolatry, unrighteousness, immorality, innocent bloodshed, and injustice.

The innocent blood of 65 million aborted babies has brought bloodguiltiness and curses upon our nation. The real total number of

---

[33] Peter J. Marshall, Jr., and David B. Manuel, Jr., The Light and the Glory: Did God have a plan for America? (Grand Rapids, MI: Fleming H. Revell, 1977), pp. 80-144.

aborted babies is inestimable and far, far higher considering the total number of years and variety of methods used (i.e., surgical, Morning After Pill, abortifacient pills, and the abortifacient nature of many contraceptives). Dr. Wm. Robert Johnston and I have invested decades systematically tracking the number of abortions in nations to create a Sacred Accounting of the babies killed. We have documents 1.4 Billion Aborted Babies worldwide between 1921 and 2023. Abortion is the Greatest Genocide in history, the number 1 cause of death worldwide, and the number 1 violation of inalienable human rights. (For the history and policies of 196 nations, and abortion data for 110 nations and 35 territories, with analysis, graphs, maps and tables, see the *Abortion Worldwide Report*, www.GLCPublications.com; and Dr. Johnston's full data at https://www.johnstonsarchive.net/policy/abortion/index.html).

Jesus weeps over the slaughter of the innocents. Yet astonishingly, for every person who genuinely repents, He covers their sin with His shed blood and righteousness. If we humble ourselves and repent as a nation, we can be assured of God's forgiveness and mercy in judgment, and have hope for restoration of religious and civil liberty.

## Bible study:

1. Is there one true God or many gods (Exodus 20:1-6; Deuteronomy 4:31-39; Isaiah 45:5-7, 21-22; 46:9)?

   ................................................................................................................

2. Who alone are we commanded to worship and serve (Exodus 3:12; 23:25; Deuteronomy 6:13; Psalm 2:11-12; 22:23-31; 86:8-10; 96:1-13)?

   ................................................................................................................

3. Who are we commanded not to worship and serve (Exodus 20:3-5; 23:23-24; Deuteronomy 6:14-15)?

   ................................................................................................................

4. What was the reason God told Moses to tell Pharoah why Egypt must let God's people go (Exodus 5:1, 3; 7:16)?

   .........................................................................................................

5. Why do you think God promised to give Abraham, Isaac, Jacob and their descendants their own land to build the nation of Israel, and reiterated the promise to Moses (Genesis 12:1-3, 7; 13:14-17; 15:7, 13-21; 17:8; 24:7; 26:1-5; 28:1-15; Exodus 6:2-8)?

   .........................................................................................................

6. Could Israel freely and fully worship and serve God while in bondage in Egypt?

   .........................................................................................................

7. Why is it important to have a place, a home, a church, and land to freely worship God?

   .........................................................................................................

8. Why is it important to have a community and nation where you can live out your Christian faith without danger to yourself, your family, your church, or your work?

   .........................................................................................................

9. How does the Bible define "Pure and undefiled religion" in James 1:27?

   .........................................................................................................

## QUESTIONS FOR CONTEMPLATION OR DISCUSSION:

1. In the 1620 Mayflower Compact, what did the Pilgrims declare was their purpose in coming to America and establishing a settlement at the risk of their lives?

   .........................................................................................................

2. What did Governor William Bradford write that further explained their purpose?

   .........................................................................................................

3.  What God-given inalienable rights were violated that drove people to come to the American Colonies?

    ..................................................................................................

4.  Why were the American Colonies viewed as "an Asylum for liberty, civil and religious"?

    ..................................................................................................

5.  What did Rev. Adams say was their noble purpose, and what was it not?

    ..................................................................................................

6.  Rev. West observed that God "designed this continent to be the asylum of liberty and true religion." What is true religion?

    ..................................................................................................

7.  What are some differences between the Jamestown and Plymouth settlements, and how are some of those same conflicting trends evident today?

    ..................................................................................................

8.  What is needed to restore the nation to being an "asylum for liberty and true religion"?

    ..................................................................................................

## SERMON OUTLINE SUGGESTION:

1.  Why did the Pilgrims come to America?
2.  How did the Pilgrims at Plymouth differ from most of the men who founded Jamestown?
3.  If America was settled primarily as an "asylum for liberty and true religion," how can we restore our nation to its original noble purpose?

# CHAPTER FIVE

# Freedom of Mind, Conscience, and Religion

THE AMERICAN COLONISTS FIRMLY BELIEVED THAT FREEDOM of thought, conscience, and religion are inalienable human rights bestowed by God the Creator on every person. They cherished these divine gifts more than life itself. Because the Creator writes His Law upon the hearts and minds of every person (Psalm 40:8; Jeremiah 31:33; Acts 10:34-35; Romans 1:18-20; 2:1-16; Hebrews 8:10; 10:16), freedom of conscience is essential to live in right relationship and obedience to Him, and in right relationship to one another.

Therefore, the right structuring of society for righteousness and liberty first requires that individuals be free to think, believe in, obey and worship God; express their thoughts, opinions and beliefs; and live in obedience to authorities and civil law, all without violation of their consciences. Second, this right structuring requires that parents be free to instruct their children, and the clergy and Church be free to instruct families, officials, and society so they know the truth and how to live consistent with the will of God. Third, it requires that the civil government create and enforce laws consistent with the Laws of Nature and of Nature's God, and protecting these sacred rights. Further, these rights can only be preserved if those who *abuse* the rights are punished. This is the only way a community or nation can be structured so that individuals, families, clergy, businessmen, employers, employees, and officials are able to live consistent with their consciences, in harmony with one another, and not be compelled to believe or do something against a rightly informed conscience.

In 1762, only three years prior to the infamous Stamp Act, Rev. Abraham Williams (1726-1784), pastor of the Congregational Church of Sandwich, Massachusetts, delivered *An Election Sermon* before the Governor and General Court of Massachusetts in Boston. Rev. Williams conveyed the dominant views on the rights of conscience and religion held in the Colonies during the seventeenth and eighteenth centuries.

> Human Laws can't control the Mind. — The Rights
> of Conscience, are unalienable; inseparable from our
> Nature; — they ought not — they cannot possibly be
> given up to Society. Therefore *Religion, as it consists*
> in *right Sentiments, Affections*, and *Behaviour* towards
> God, — as it is chiefly *internal* and *private*, can be
> regulated only by God Himself.[34]

Rev. William Gordon, in his sermon at the Boston Lecture in 1774, commented on the "favorable circumstances" that prepared Americans for the responsible use of freedom.

> Here allow me to run through a brief summary of
> those favorable circumstances . . . the increasing
> acquaintance with the rights of conscience in matters
> of religion, as belonging equally alike to men of all
> parties and denominations, while they conduct as
> good members of civil society, without endeavoring
> to injure their neighbors of different or opposite
> sentiments . . . .

---

[34] Abraham Williams, pastor, Congregational Church of Sandwich, Massachusetts, "An Election Sermon, Delivered before the Governor and General Court of Massachusetts" (Boston, 1762). Reprinted in op. cit., American Political Writing During the Founding Era, 1760-1805, 1:8.

> The rights of conscience are too sacred for any civil
> power on earth to interdict . . . (It is) necessary and
> essential, to guard against . . . unnatural alliances
> between church and state, the sword of the Spirit and
> the sword of the magistrate.[35]

The Church bears the "sword of the Spirit," which is the Word of God, the Bible (Hebrews 4:12), and is "the pillar and support of the truth" (1 Timothy 3:15). It is *not* an instrument of force, but of spirit. During prior centuries, when the Church took up arms against enemies for spiritual reasons, insofar as it did, it ceased to represent Christ and be the Church. Nevertheless, there is always an individual, community and national right to self-defense, and of repelling and crushing an enemy who attacks and seeks to destroy human life or steal land or property that does not belong to him. But matters of "the spirit" pertain to the mind, conscience, and religion.

The State bears the "sword of the magistrate," which is the lawful use of force to maintain order and punish those who do evil (Romans 13:3-4). It *is* an instrument of force. The very nature of the State is to use force to uphold civil law. The State implements its programs by force, or the threat of force. This is appropriate as long as it is for the purpose of justice, maintaining order, and is not excessive, especially by punishing those whose actions are truly evil and deadly or harmful to others.

Consequently, as Dr. Gordon recognized, the "rights of conscience" are sacred and can be preserved only if the government does not interfere with them. If the civil power seeks to control matters of mind, conscience, and religion, it will by nature use force to require compliance with its views, thus trampling upon those sacred human rights. An "unnatural alliance" is created when the State controls, or seeks to control, such matters in the lives of individuals, families,

---

[35] Op. cit., William Gordon, "A Discourse Preached on . . . the day recommended by Provincial Congress," pp. 214-215, see note, p. 216.

churches, ministries, schools, education, businesses, or organizations, and gains their cooperation or compliance.

Rev. Samuel West, in his 1776 sermon to the public officials of the Colony of Massachusetts-Bay, explained how our consciences work and how this proves that "the Deity is our supreme magistrate."

> The Deity has also invested us with moral powers and faculties, by which we are enabled to discern the difference between right and wrong, truth and falsehood, good and evil: hence the approbation of mind that arises upon doing a good action, and the remorse of conscience which we experience when we counteract the moral sense and do that which is evil. This proves that, in what is commonly called a state of nature, we are the subjects of the divine law and government; that the Deity is our supreme magistrate, who has written His law in our hearts, and will reward or punish us according as we obey or disobey His commands.[36]

Later in the same sermon, Rev. West said that the liberty of expression was "a blessing of Heaven." As a gift from Heaven, proper exercises of liberty are always consistent with the will of God, and abuses of liberty are contrary to His will. To preserve liberty, civil authorities must punish those who abuse their liberty, that is, by acting in ways that violate civil law. Rev. West concluded,

> I cannot but look upon it as a peculiar blessing of Heaven that we live in a land where every one can freely deliver his sentiments upon religious subjects, and have the privilege of worshipping God according to the dictates of his own conscience, without any molestation or disturbance—a privilege which I

---

[36] Op. cit., Samuel West, "A Sermon Preached before the Honorable Council, and Honorable House of Representatives," pp. 267, 299-300.

hope we shall ever keep up and strenuously maintain. No principles ought ever to be discounted by civil authority but such as tend to the subversion of the state. So long as a man is a good member of society, he is accountable to God alone for his religious sentiments; but when men are found disturbers of the public peace, stirring up sedition, or practicing against the state, no pretense of religion or conscience ought to screen them from being brought to condign punishment.[37]

Rev. John Leland (1754-1841) was a Baptist pastor from Virginia and Massachusetts, who preached and wrote publicly about religious liberty. In a booklet titled, *The Rights of Conscience Inalienable, and therefore Religious Opinions not cognizable by Law,* he defined conscience and made four assertions:

"Are the Rights of Conscience alienable, or inalienable?" . . . The word conscience signifies

---

[37] Ibid.

common science, a court of judicature which the Almighty has erected in every human breast: a censor morum over all his conduct. Conscience will ever judge right, when it is rightly informed; and speak the truth when it understands it. . . .

1. Every man must give an account of himself to God, and therefore every man ought to be at liberty to serve God in that way that he can best reconcile it to his conscience. If Government, can answer for individuals at the day of judgment, let men be controlled by it, in religious matters; otherwise, let men be free.

2. It would be sinful for a man to surrender that to man, which is to be kept sacred for God. A man's mind should be always open to conviction; and an honest man will receive that doctrine which appears the best demonstrated: and what is more common than for the best of men to change their minds? Such are the prejudices of the mind, and such the force of tradition, that a man who never alters his mind, is either very weak or very stubborn. How painful then must it be to an honest heart, to be bound to observe the principles of his former belief, after he is convinced of their imbecility? And this ever has, and ever will be the case, while the rights of conscience are considered alienable. . . .

3. (S)urely it is very iniquitous to bind the consciences of (one's) children—to make fetters for them before they are born, is very cruel. . . .

4. Religion is a matter between God and individuals:
religious opinions of men not being the objects of
civil government, nor any ways under its control.[38]

Rev. Leland considered the mind of man "sacred for God." He knew that all men are fallible, and they need to "be always open to conviction" by the Spirit of God in order to realize and correct their errors. He commented on how painful "must it be to an honest heart, to be bound to observe the principles of his former belief," a belief he realized was wrong.

In 1794, writing under the pen name of Jack Nips, Rev. Leland said this in *The Yankee Spy*:

> Should a man refuse to pay his tribute for the support
> of government, or any wise disturb the peace and
> good order of civil (society), he should be punished
> according to his crime, let his religion be what it
> will; but when a man is a peaceable subject of state,
> he should be protected in worshipping the Deity
> according to the dictates of his own conscience. . . .
>
> The rights of conscience should always be considered
> inalienable—religious opinions are not the objects of
> civil government, nor any way under its jurisdiction.
> Laws should only respect civil society; then if men
> are disturbers they ought to be punished.[39]

---

[38] John Leland, "The Rights of Conscience Inalienable, and therefore Religious Opinions not cognizable by Law: or, The high-flying Church-man" (New-London: T. Green & Son, 1791), pp. 6-8; 29 pages. [LOC: BV 741 .L4 Office/Rare Book Collection]

[39] Jack Nips [John Leland (1754-1841)], Baptist pastor, Massachusetts, *The Yankee Spy* (Boston, 1794). Reprinted in, op. cit., <u>American Political Writing</u>, 2:978-989. [LOC: BV 741 .L4 Office]

Laws should *not* be made regulating how parents raise their children; how churches are governed; what parents, clergy, and educators teach; or how anyone worships God. The civil government should protect, and not interfere with, God-given liberties. But if anyone harms another person and commits a criminal act, then it is appropriate for civil authorities to intervene. If they do not intervene, they fail to fulfill their God-given duty to restrain and punish evil.

To preserve freedoms of mind, conscience and religion, it is essential to maintain the proper distinction between God-given spheres of authority and responsibility; namely, (1) individual self-government, (2) family, (3) Church and ministry, (4) business or private organizations, and (5) civil government. Dr. Francis Schaeffer told me about these spheres, and the founding generations understood and respected them, but most Americans today do not, except intuitively. For decades we have increasingly witnessed some civil authorities disregarding and violating (or supporting the violation of) inalienable rights of mind, conscience and religion. These violations have included individual rights, disregard for parental authority, threatening clergy and churches, coercing and harassing business owners who refuse to do something that would violate their consciences, firing employees for expressing their righteous beliefs or opinions, discriminating against certain organizations who have done nothing evil, etc. The invasions have become so frequent and egregious that the liberty of all Americans, and the American experiment, are at grave risk.

If we can regain the understanding that freedom of mind, conscience, and religion are inalienable rights given by God, and take the necessary steps to ensure protection of these rights, then there is hope for our nation. But if protection is not restored for these inherent rights and the right to life, which are the foundation for all other human rights, then the nation will continue its rapid spiritual, moral and cultural decline. The future of our nation hangs in the balance.

## BIBLE STUDY:

1. What did the Creator write upon the hearts and minds of every person (Psalm 40:8; Jeremiah 31:33; Acts 10:34-35; Romans 1:18-20; 2:1-16; Hebrews 8:10; 10:16)?

   ..........................................................................................................................

2. What can we learn from the example of Daniel and his three friends who, as young men, refused to violate their conscience and religion (Daniel 1:8-21)?

   ..........................................................................................................................

3. What can we learn from the example of Shadrach, Meshach and Abednego, who refused to obey the king's order to worship his image, and were thrown in the furnace of fire (Daniel 3)? Why did they say, "O Nebuchadnezzar, we do not need to give you an answer concerning this matter" (3:16)?

   ..........................................................................................................................

4. What can we learn from the example of Daniel when his opponents tried to cause his death by creating a law forbidding him to pray to anyone except the king, resulting in him being thrown into the lions' den (Daniel 6)?

   ..........................................................................................................................

5. What can we learn from the example of the apostles who were thrown in prison because of preaching Christ (Acts 5:17-42)? Why did they declare to the religious leaders, "We must obey God rather than men" (5:29)?

   ..........................................................................................................................

6. Who bears "the sword of the Spirit, which is the word of God" (Ephesians 6:17; Hebrews 4:12)?

   ..........................................................................................................................

7. Who bears "the sword" of the magistrate, a sword of force (Romans 13:3-4)?

.......................................................................................................................

8. Do matters of the mind, conscience, and religion pertain to "the spirit" or "the magistrate?"

.......................................................................................................................

## QUESTIONS FOR CONTEMPLATION OR DISCUSSION:

1. Are freedoms of mind, conscience and religion from God, man or government?

.......................................................................................................................

2. Does government have any authority to control or regulate conscience, religion, or a person's mind?

.......................................................................................................................

3. What did Rev. Williams say about human laws?

.......................................................................................................................

4. What sword does the church hold?

.......................................................................................................................

5. What sword does the magistrate/state/government hold?

.......................................................................................................................

6. Rev. West described how our conscience works, saying this proves that God, not government, is the "supreme magistrate" over our minds. What do you think?

.......................................................................................................................

7. Why did Rev. Leland say our minds are "sacred for God?"

.......................................................................................................................

8. When is it correct and necessary for civil government to intervene?

...............................................................................................................................

## SERMON OUTLINE SUGGESTION:

1. What are freedoms of mind, conscience and religion?
2. Who gave and who has authority over these inalienable liberties?
3. What is the authority of the Church and authority of government in these matters?
4. What must we do to preserve or restore these God-given liberties?

# CHAPTER SIX

# Not All Sins are Crimes

NOTHER DISTINCTION BETWEEN CIVIL AND NON-CIVIL matters essential to the preservation of liberty is the difference between sins and crimes. All crime is sin, but not all sins are crimes. Civil power is only to be exercised in civil and criminal matters. A person may think about stealing an item, and be tempted to do so, but he would only commit a crime if he stole the item. Contemplation of a crime is a sin, but not a crime; that is, unless one threatens to commit a serious crime and there is evidence that he is taking steps to carry out that threat (e.g., start a fire, threaten to murder, terrorism).

This distinction between sins and crimes corresponds to that between thoughts and actions. Many actions are sins, but not crimes. The source of sin is mankind's inherent fallen, sinful nature, which leads to wrong ways of thinking and acting (Genesis 3; Psalm 14:1-3; 53:1-3; Jeremiah 17:9; Mark 10:18; Luke 18:19). Every person is accountable to God for every sin, but not to civil government. If a crime is committed, then it is a matter for the civil government.

In 1780, during the War for Independence against the most powerful military on earth, with the outcome uncertain, Rev. Simeon Howard, D.D. (1733-1804) preached an election sermon to the Council and House of Representatives of the State of Massachusetts-Bay, concluding with this warning and appeal:

> Let me now conclude by reminding this assembly
> in general that it concerns us all to fear God, and to
> be men of truth, hating covetousness. The low and
> declining state of religion and virtue among us is

too obvious not to be seen, and of too threatening an aspect not to be lamented, by all the lovers of God and their country. Though our happiness as a community depends much upon the conduct of our rulers, yet it is not in the power of the best government to make impious, profligate people happy. How well soever our public affairs may be managed, we may undo ourselves by our vices. And it is from hence, I apprehend, that our greatest danger arises. That spirit of infidelity, selfishness, luxury, and dissipation, which so deeply marks our present manners, is more formidable than all the arms of our enemies. Would we but reform our evil ways, humble ourselves under the corrections, and be thankful for the mercies of Heaven; revive that piety and public spirit, that temperance and frugality, which have entailed immortal honor on the memory of our renowned ancestors; we might, then, putting our trust in God, humbly hope that our public calamities would be soon at an end, our independence established, our rights and liberties secured, and glory, peace, and happiness dwell in our land. Such happy effects to the public might we expect from a general reformation.[40]

Dr. Howard knew that public officials could not change the hearts of men, but these leaders could reform their own personal lives with the help of God, and set a good example. It is sinful to be

---

[40] Simeon Howard, A.M., pastor of the West Church in Boston, "A Sermon Preached Before the Honorable Council, and the Honorable House of Representatives of the State of Massachusetts-Bay, in New-England, May 31, 1780. Being the anniversary for the election of the honorable council" (Boston: printed by John Gill, 1780). Reprinted in op. cit., Pulpit of the American Revolution, p. 395; full sermon: pp. 355-398.

selfish, covetous and meditate on impure things, but these are vices, not crimes. Only "a general reformation" can set both officials and citizens free from vices that lead to crimes.

In 1794, Rev. John Leland wrote an article in *The Yankee Spy*, calling for an amendment to the *Constitution of Massachusetts*. He believed the legislators had made an error when they failed to distinguish between sins and crimes and made worshipping God a civil duty.

> What leads legislators into this error, is confounding *sins* and *crimes* together—making no difference between *moral evil* and *state rebellion*, not considering that a man may be infected with moral evil, and yet be guilty of no crime, punishable by law. If a man worships one God, three Gods, twenty Gods, or no God—if he pays adoration one day in a week, seven days, or no day—wherein does he injure the life, liberty or property of another. Let any or all these actions be supposed to be religious evils of an enormous size, yet they are not crimes to be punished by the laws of state, which extend no further, in justice, than to punish the man who works ill to his neighbor. . . .
>
> (V)olumes . . . have been written, to show the havoc among men the principle of mixing *sins* and *crimes* together has effected, while men in power have taken their own opinions as infallible tests of right and wrong.[41]

Rev. Leland held that civil government should *not* punish citizens for sins that are not also crimes, for what is "moral evil," but not "state

---

[41] Op. cit., Jack Nips [John Leland], *The Yankee Spy*.

rebellion." He continued by identifying certain responsibilities of citizens, and addressing the matter of motive in crimes.

It is well noticed that none shall be protected by law, but those who properly demean themselves as peaceable subjects of the commonwealth. This, however, should be extended to all men, as well as to Christian denominations.

For any man, or set of men, to expect protection from the law, when they do not subject themselves to government, is a vain expectation. Let a man's motive be what it may, let him have what object soever in view; if his practice is opposed to good law, he is to be punished. Magistrates are not to consult his motive or object, but his actions. . . .

(F)or instances, we shall pay attention to a few recent transactions of our own. A Shaking-Quaker, in a violent manner, cast his wife into a mill-pond in cold weather; his plea was, that God ordered him so to do. Now the question is, Ought he not to be punished as much as if he had done the deed in anger? Was not the abuse to the woman as great? Could the magistrate perfectly know whether it was God, Satan, or ill-will, that prompted him to do the deed? The answers to these questions are easy.

In the year of 1784, Matthew Womble, of Virginia, killed his wife and four sons, in obedience to a Shining One, who, he said, was the Son of God, to merit heaven by the action; but if the court had been fearful of offending that Shining One, and pitied Womble's soul, they would never have inflicted that punishment upon him which they did the October following. Neither his motive, which was obedience, nor his object, which was the salvation of his soul had any weight on the jury.

Should magistrates or jurors be biased by such protestations, the most atrocious villains would always pass with impunity . . . .[42]

A criminal act is a criminal act, even if the perpetrator believed he had good motives. On the other hand, a man whose beliefs do not agree with government policy, but who does not harm others, should not be disturbed.

The motive of one committing a crime does not change the fact that he committed a crime. He ought to be judged according to the law for his crime, which is why our statues representing "justice" wear blindfolds. The civil authority must judge the criminal act, and punish the criminal for it. The judge and jury can take into account what he said and did, but can never know with certainty his thoughts and motives.

There is one aspect that is vitally important to determine, and can involve assessing thoughts or motives: intent. Did the person who committed the crime do so with intent, or was it an accident? If it was not intentional, then the penalty should be significantly lower (see Exodus 21:12-14; Numbers 35:10-34; Deuteronomy 19:1-13).

God will hold a criminal accountable for his sinful thoughts, motives and actions—both those he had when contemplating and when committing the crime. God alone knows a man's heart and can judge it. If the civil authority does its duty well, the criminal will face accountability for his crime; yet even more importantly, will hopefully recognize that he will be held accountable before the Highest Court on the Day of Judgment. The criminal can repent and receive God's

---

[42] Ibid.

forgiveness through Christ's sacrifice for his sins, and not face eternal punishment for them, regardless of whatever punishment he must endure here on Earth – just like the repentant thief on the cross next to Jesus.

## BIBLE STUDY:

1. What is sin? (Look up Hebrew and Greek words for "sin.")

2. What is the source of sin (Genesis 3; Psalm 14:1-3; 53:1-3; Jeremiah 17:9; Mark 10:18; Luke 18:19)?

3. Who has jurisdiction over sin (Psalm 51)?

4. What is a crime?

5. Who has jurisdiction over crimes?

6. Which of the sins listed in the 10 Commandments might also come under government authority (Exodus 20:1-17)?

7. Does the Bible clarify what sins are crimes that come under government authority (e.g., murder or manslaughter: Genesis 9:6; Exodus 21:12-23; Numbers 35:10-34)?

## QUESTIONS FOR CONTEMPLATION OR DISCUSSION:

1. Are all sins also crimes?

2. Are all crimes also sins?

   .........................................................................................

3. Does civil government have authority over sins or crimes?

   .........................................................................................

4. Why can civil government not make people righteous, good or happy?

   .........................................................................................

5. What are dangers of treating "sins and crimes" the same?

   .........................................................................................

6. What is the difference between motive and intent, and which should concern a judge or jury?

   .........................................................................................

7. If human authorities and governments do their job of holding a person accountable for a crime, do you think this will likely cause the criminal to realize his ultimate accountability to God, and create an opportunity for repentance and forgiveness?

   .........................................................................................

## SERMON OUTLINE SUGGESTION:

1. What is sin?
2. What is a crime?
3. What are the dangers of mixing or confusing sins and crimes?
4. How does avoiding this confusion create a free society and just government?

# CHAPTER SEVEN

# Religion and Government

G REAT CONFUSION EXISTS TODAY REGARDING THE ROLE OF religion in civil government, between the spheres of church and state. A proper understanding of the distinct spheres took generations, even centuries, to develop. The colonists and Founding Fathers of the United States of America, like others in Europe, finally discerned that anything pertaining to religion, beliefs, the mind, freedom of thought, conscience, freedom of speech, and the church itself, were entirely outside the jurisdiction of civil government. They also recognized the necessity of true religion and liberty to cultivating good citizens and leaders, and establishing free forms of government. They defined true religion as the Judeo-Christian religion and worldview.[43]

In 1771, Rev. John Tucker (1719-1792) of Massachusetts, in an *Election Day Sermon*, identified several characteristics necessary to producing good citizens and good public officials.

> True religion:—A sacred reverence of the Deity:—
> The love of virtue and goodness, are as necessary
> to make good subjects, as good Rulers: And a spirit
> of liberty is requisite, to render obedience true and
> genuine both to God and man.[44]

---

[43] Op. cit., Noah Webster, <u>An American Dictionary of the English Language</u>, s.v. "Religion."

[44] John Tucker, pastor of First Church in Newbury, Massachusetts, "Election Day Sermon" (Boston, 1771). Reprinted in op. cit., <u>American Political Writing</u>, 1:171.

True religion brings good order to society as it requires virtue and encourages goodness and voluntary obedience to Almighty God and lawful human authorities. Rev. Tucker recognized that obedience must be voluntary to be genuine. When people choose to obey human authorities out of reverence for God and "love of virtue and goodness," then they can establish and maintain a free form of government. They must first be self-governing, and be virtuous enough to do what is right without coercion. However, if their public officials fail to uphold the law or are corrupt, and the people refuse to obey the law voluntarily, it will be impossible for them to preserve a free and limited government.

Rev. Samuel West, in a 1776 sermon to public officials, explained why civil government is needed.

> The Great Creator, having designed the human race for society, has made us dependent on one another for happiness. He has so constituted us that it becomes both our duty and interest to seek the public good....
>
> The necessity of forming ourselves into politic bodies, and granting to our rulers a power to enact laws for the public safety, and to enforce them by proper penalties, arises from our being in a fallen and degenerate state . . . (C)ivil government is absolutely necessary for the peace and safety of mankind; and, consequently, that all good magistrates, while they faithfully discharge the trust reposed in them, ought to be religiously and conscientiously obeyed.[45]

We need civil government because every person is "in a fallen and degenerate state." We are all guilty of sinful thoughts, attitudes, and

---

[45] Op. cit., Samuel West, "A Sermon Preached before the Honorable Council, and the Honorable House of Representatives," p. 267-268.

actions (though only actions, or threats, are within the jurisdiction of civil government). Sometimes it is only the fear of punishment that restrains us from doing evil. This is why Rev. West said that "civil government is absolutely necessary for the peace and safety of mankind." If we are going to live together in peace, and as God designed us to, then we must have some means of maintaining order and punishing those who do wrong.

Dr. Samuel Stillman was a man of integrity sent by the people of Massachusetts to the Convention in 1779 to form the state constitution. He was again sent to the state convention in 1788, where he made significant contributions toward adoption of the *United States Constitution.* Prior to the convention of 1779, Dr. Stillman delivered a sermon before the Council and House of Representatives of the State of Massachusetts Bay, titled, *The Duty of Magistrates.* He also explained the important and good effect of the Church upon society.

"Thus saith [Jesus] unto them, Render therefore unto Caesar the things that are Caesar's, and unto God the things that are God's" (Matthew 22:21)....

I shall therefore proceed to apply this sacred passage to ourselves, in our present situation, by considering:

I. What those duties are which the people owe to the civil magistrate.

II. The duties of the magistrate to the people. And then,

III. Endeavor to draw the line between the things that belong to Caesar, and those things that belong to God....

With us, it is a first and fundamental principle, that God made all men equal... And as they are equal, so they are likewise in a state of entire freedom.

From the premises, the following is a natural conclusion—*That the authority of the civil magistrate is, under God, derived from the people.*[46]

Dr. Stillman identified the "first and fundamental principle that God made all men equal." Consequently, civil authority must be "derived from the people."

From hence arises, in my view, the indispensable necessity of a BILL OF RIGHTS drawn up in the most explicit language, previously to the ratification of a constitution of government; which should contain its fundamental principles.[47]

A bill of rights recognizes that the people have unalienable rights from God, and that their government derives its power from them – the people. It is in their best interest to ensure that their government protects, and does not violate, their unalienable rights. Dr. Stillman thought that the pattern set in the other State constitutions, and in the national charter (the *Declaration of Independence*), ought to be

---

[46] Op. cit., Samuel Stillman, "The Duty of Magistrates."
[47] Ibid.

followed by Massachusetts. He believed the people of Massachusetts needed a bill of rights that contained "explicit language" protecting their unalienable rights based upon "fundamental principle(s)" inviolable by civil government. He continued:

> Some of those principles which, I apprehend, may be called *fundamental* (include):
>
> - That the great end for which men enter into a state of civil society is their own advantage.
> - That civil rulers, as they derive their authority from the people, so they are accountable to them for the use they make of it.
> - The elections ought to be *free* and *frequent*.
> - That representation should be as equal as possible.
> - That as all men are equal by nature, so, when they enter into a state of civil government, they are entitled precisely to the same rights and privileges, or to an equal degree of political happiness.
> - That some of the natural rights of mankind are unalienable, and subject to no control but that of the Deity. Such are the SACRED RIGHTS of CONSCIENCE; which, in a state of nature and of civil society, are exactly the same. They can neither be parted with nor controlled by any human authority whatever ....
> - That no laws are obligatory on the people but those that have obtained a like consent. Nor are such laws of any force, if, proceeding from a corrupt majority of the legislature, they are incompatible with the fundamental principles of government, and tend to subvert it.[48]

Dr. Stillman later addressed the "all-important rights of conscience," and quoted John Locke (1632-1704) "to distinguish

---

[48] Ibid.

exactly the business of civil government from that of religion." The significant quotes from Locke reveal Dr. Stillman's reliance upon his writings.

> It becomes us, therefore, to settle this most weighty matter in our different forms of government, in such a manner, that no occasion may be left in future for the violation of the all-important rights of conscience....

> "I esteem it," says the justly-celebrated Mr. Locke, "above all things, necessary to distinguish exactly the business of civil government from that of religion....

> "First, because the care of souls is not committed to the civil magistrate . . . because it appears not that God has ever given any such authority to one man over another, as to compel any one to his religion ... All the life and power of true religion consist in the inward and full persuasion of the mind; and faith is not faith without believing.

> "In the second place. The care of souls cannot belong to the civil magistrate, because his power consists only in outward force; but true and saving religion consists in the inward persuasion of the mind, without which nothing can be acceptable to God.

> "In the third place, the care of the salvation of men's souls cannot belong to the civil magistrate, because, though the rigor of laws and the force of penalties were capable to convince and change men's minds, yet would not that help at all to the salvation of their souls; for, there being but one truth, one way to heaven, what hope is there that more men would be

led into it if they had no other rule to follow but the religion of the court, and were put under the necessity to quit the light of their own reason, to oppose the dictates of their own consciences, and blindly resign up themselves to the will of their governors . . . ."

These sentiments . . . discover a true greatness and liberality of mind, and are calculated properly to limit the power of civil rulers, and to secure to every man the inestimable right of private judgment.[49]

Dr. Stillman then spoke of the positive influence of the Church upon society.

(T)he *kingdom of Christ* . . . we mean His church . . . does not in any respect interfere with civil government, but rather tends to promote its peace and happiness, because its subjects are taught to obey the magistracy, and to *lead peaceable and quiet lives in all godliness and honesty.* . . . They use no other force than that of reason and argument.[50]

Rev. John Leland wrote a booklet quoted earlier, titled, *The Rights of Conscience Inalienable, and therefore Religious Opinions not cognizable by Law.* Rev. Leland discussed four types of foundations of civil government. The fourth, a constitution (i.e., compact), is consistent with the fundamental principles delineated by Dr. Stillman above.

There are four principles contended for, as the foundation of civil government, viz. Birth, property, grace, and compact. The first of these is practiced

---

[49] Ibid.
[50] Ibid.

upon in all hereditary monarchies; where it is believed that the son of a monarch is entitled to dominion, upon the decease of his father, whether he be a wise man or a fool. The second principle is built upon, in all aristocratical governments, where the rich landholders have the sole rule of all their tenants; and make laws, at pleasure, which are binding upon all. The third principle is adopted by those kingdoms and states, that require a religious test to qualify an officer of state proscribing all non-conformists from civil and religious liberty. This is the error of Constantine's government, who first established the Christian religion by law, and then proscribed the Pagans, and banished the Arian heretics. . . .

The same evil has twisted itself into the British form of government; where, in the state establishment of the church of England, no man is eligible to any office, civil or military, without he subscribes to the 39 articles and book of common prayer; and even then, upon receiving a commission for the army, the law obliges him to receive the sacrament of the LORD's supper: and no nonconformist is allowed the liberty of his conscience, without he subscribes to all the 39 articles but about four. And when that is done, his purse strings are drawn by others, to pay preachers, in whom he puts no confidence, and whom he never hears.

This was the case of several of the Southern States (until the revolution), in which the church of England was established. . . . The fourth principle (compact) is adopted in the American States, as the basis of

civil government.—This foundation appears to be
a just one.[51]

Rev. Leland explained why a constitution (a civil covenant or compact) is the best foundation for civil government. He provided a parable of a man who went to an island, and had 10 sons. One went vagrant, so they set up a system of democratic justice, with each man having one vote. This was feasible with a small population. However, when the population grew to 9,000, such a system of justice was impractical. Thus, they established a representative system by which each man still retained one vote, but did not retain direct civil governing power. They elected civil magistrates to represent them and conduct the affairs of government, which is a *republican* form of government. Leland continued:

From this simple parable, the following things are demonstrated.

1.  That the law was not made for the righteous man, but for the disobedient.
2.  That righteous men have to part with a little of their liberty and property to preserve the rest.
3.  That all power is vested in, and consequently derived from the people.
4.  That the law should rule over rulers, and not rulers over the law.
5.  That government is founded in compact.
6.  That every law made by the legislators, inconsistent with the compact, modernly called a constitution, is usurpive in the legislators, and not binding on the people.
7.  That whenever government is found inadequate to preserve the liberty and property of the people, they have an indubitable right to alter it, so as to answer those purposes.

---

[51] Op. cit., John Leland, "The Rights of Conscience Inalienable," pp. 3-6.

8.   That legislators, in their legislative capacity, cannot alter the constitution, for they are hired servants of the people, to act within the limits of the constitution.[52]

Colonial Americans learned these truths the hard way, namely, through abuses of power that caused the loss of life, liberty, and property, both in Europe and in the Colonies. This was *not* just theory to them. They set up forms of government to prevent the same abuses.

Rev. Timothy Stone delivered *An Election Sermon* in 1792. He demonstrated how the relationship between true religion and good government is inseverable, and how in numerous ways the religion of Jesus Christ is the highest glory of every man and nation; that the Spirit of Christ is the source of liberty.

> The holy religion of the Son of GOD, hath a most powerful and benign influence upon moral beings in society. It not only restrains malicious revengeful passions, and curbs unruly lusts; but will in event, eradicate them all from the human breast—it implants all the divine graces and social virtues in the heart—it sweetens the dispositions of men, and fits them for all the pleasing satisfactions, of rational friendship—teaches them self denial—inspires them with a generous public spirit—fills them with love to others, to righteousness and mercy—makes them careful to discharge the duties of their stations—diligent and contented in their callings—this, beyond any other consideration, will increase the real dignity of rulers—will give quiet and submission to subjects—this is the only true and genuine spirit of liberty, which can give abiding union and energy to states—and will enable them to

---

[52]   Ibid.

bear prosperity without pride—and support them in adversity without dejection—this will afford all classes of men consolation in death, and render them happy in GOD, their full eternal portion, in the coming world.

Religion, therefore is the glory of all intelligent beings, from the highest angel, to the meanest of the human race; and will for ever happify its possessors, considered, either individually, or, as connected in society.[53]

Rev. Stone continued by clarifying the direct and "happy connection between religion and good government."

If the preceding observations, have their foundation in reason, and the word of GOD: we see the happy connection between religion and good government. The idea that there is, and ought to be, no connection between religion and civil policy, appears to rest upon this absurd supposition: that men by entering into society for mutual advantage, become quite a different class of beings from what they were before, that they cease to be moral beings; and consequently, lose their relation and obligations to GOD, as creatures and subjects; and also their relations to each other as rational social creatures. If these are the real consequences of civil connections, they are unhappy indeed, as they must exceedingly debase and degrade human nature; and it is readily acknowledged, these things being true, that religion can have no further demands upon them. But, if none of the relations or obligations of men to their Creator, and each other

---

[53] Op. cit., Timothy Stone, "An Election Sermon."

are lost by entering society; if they still remain moral and accountable beings, and, if religion is the glory and perfection of moral beings, then the connection between religion and good government is evident— and all attempts to separate them are unfriendly to society, and inimical to good government, and must originate in ignorance or bad design.[54]

The separation of church and state theory that is prominent today, is contrary to our forefathers understanding of the relationship between religion and government. Every man who serves in public office takes with him his convictions and views, religious and otherwise. His actions, policies, and votes will always reveal what he truly believes, not necessarily what he says. If his beliefs are consistent with those of the Judeo-Christian religion – and thus consistent with the views of most of our forefathers who were careful guardians of our liberties, working diligently to keep the government within its lawful limits – then his policies will have a good effect on our nation. If his beliefs are contrary to these, and he refuses to restrain his powers to constitutional limits, then he is a tyrant and his policies will have bad effects on our nation; and we should not elect, nor fail to remove such persons from public office, including justices and judges.

Rev. Stone believed that true religion would have a good effect on government. During President George Washington's first term, Stone described the glorious nation that America could become (and did become), if it allowed true religion to have its proper effect on civil government.

> Religion essentially consists in friendly affection to GOD, and His rational offspring; and such affection, can never injure that government which hath public happiness for its object . . . A civil community,

---

[54] Ibid.

formed, organized, and administered, agreeably to the principles which have been suggested, will possess internal peace and energy; its strength and wealth may easily be collected for necessary defence, consequently will ever be prepared to repel foreign injuries; it will enjoy prosperity within itself, and become respectable amongst the nations of the earth.[55]

Rev. Thomas Dunn delivered a speech in 1794 to the New York Society assisting immigrants, during President Washington's second term, saying:

RELIGION is a great system of benevolence; it disposes us to consult and promote the interest and happiness of the whole family of mankind.—So far Religion and Politics are connected together.[56]

True religion is the best friend of a righteous and free government, but civil government should never in any way control it. If people want to be free, they must first build their spiritual foundations in true religion, self-government, and liberty. The family and the Church are the proper institutions for building these foundations in the minds and hearts of children, youth, and adults. Indeed, the destiny of the nation depends upon their success in doing so. God gave parents the responsibility to educate their children, and appointed the Church as "the pillar and support of the truth" (1 Timothy 3:15).

---

[55] Ibid.

[56] Op. cit., Thomas Dunn, "A Discourse, Delivered before the New York Society for the Information and Assistance of Persons Emigrating from Foreign Countries."

## BIBLE STUDY:

1. Who did God give authority and responsibility to teach the Word of God and truth (Deuteronomy 4:1-14; 6:1-25; 11:18; Joshua 8:33-35; Ezra 7:10; Nehemiah 8:1-13; Psalm 78:1-8; Matthew 28:18-20; Acts 1:8; 2:42; 6:2-4; 1 Timothy 3:15; 4:11; 2 Timothy 2:2)?

   ................................................................................................................

2. Who did God give authority and responsibility to teach children the Word of God and truth (Deuteronomy 4:9-10; 6:2, 7, 20-25; 11:18-21; Psalm 78:4-8; Proverbs 22:6; Ephesians 6:4; Hebrews 12:9)?

   ................................................................................................................

3. Review the Biblical basis for Rev. Leland's eight principles:

   (1) "That the law was not made for the righteous man, but for the disobedient" (1 Timothy 1:9).

   (2) "That righteous men have to part with a little of their liberty and property to preserve the rest" (e.g., this is required whenever anyone enters into a covenant with God or people, including the exclusivity and faithfulness of marriage, and the loyalty and tax obligations that come with national covenants).

   (3) "That all power is vested in, and consequently derived from the people" (Deuteronomy 16:16-20; e.g., although Saul and David were anointed to be rulers over Israel, neither became king until they were chosen by the people and made a covenant with them: 1 Samuel 10:17, 24-25; 2 Samuel 2:1-4; 5:1-4).

   (4) "That the law should rule over rulers, and not rulers over the law" (2 Samuel 5:3-4; 2 Kings 11:17; 22:8-13; 23:1-3, 25).

   (5) "That government is founded in compact" (see verses for #3 and #4 above).

(6) "That every law made by the legislators, inconsistent with the compact, modernly called a constitution, is usurpive [seize and control without rightful authority] in the legislators, and not binding on the people" (Psalm 94:20-21; 50:16-23; 58:1-2; Amos 6:12).

(7) "That whenever government is found inadequate to preserve the liberty and property of the people, they have an indubitable right to alter it, so as to answer those purposes" (e.g., God delivered His people out from slavery in Egypt and the oppressions of Pharoah and his government).

(8) "That legislators, in their legislative capacity, cannot alter the constitution, for they are hired servants of the people, to act within the limits of the constitution" (e.g., God rejected Saul from being king because he exercised the office reserved for the prophet and priest, and violated the covenant: 1 Samuel 13:1-14).

4. Jesus said, "Render therefore unto Caesar the things that are Caesar's, and unto God the things that are God's" (Matthew 22:21). How does His command apply to you?

..................................................................................................................

## QUESTIONS FOR CONTEMPLATION OR DISCUSSION:

1. What did Rev. West say was the cause for "The necessity of forming ourselves into politic bodies," and why "civil government is absolutely necessary?"

..................................................................................................................

2. What is necessary to preserve a free and limited government?

..................................................................................................................

3. What did Dr. Stillman say was the foundation of the principle: *"That the authority of the civil magistrate is, under God, derived from the people"*?

   .........................................................................................................................

4. Why is a Bill of Rights fundamental and essential?

   .........................................................................................................................

5. Why did Dr. Stillman call some rights "SACRED RIGHTS"?

   .........................................................................................................................

6. Why did John Locke say: "I esteem it, above all things, necessary to distinguish exactly the business of civil government from that of religion"?

   .........................................................................................................................

7. Many Christians describe Christianity as a "relationship," not a religion, saying God is not a religion. True or False? What do you think?

   .........................................................................................................................

8. What was one of the reasons John Locke said: "the care of souls is not committed to the civil magistrate?"

   .........................................................................................................................

9. What did Dr. Stillman mean when he said that the Church, "the *kingdom of Christ* . . . does not in any respect interfere with civil government, but rather tends to promote its peace and happiness?"

   .........................................................................................................................

10. What did Rev. Leland say were the four different types of principles or foundations upon which people create a civil government?

   .........................................................................................................................

11. Which of these four was "adopted in the American States, as the basis of civil government?"

..................................................................................................................................

12. What is "a *republican* form of government?"

..................................................................................................................................

13. What did Rev. Stone mean when he said, "The holy religion of the Son of GOD . . . is the glory of all intelligent beings" (e.g., good and deeply profound effects upon citizens and rulers?

..................................................................................................................................

14. What is the "happy connection between religion and good government?"

..................................................................................................................................

15. What did Rev. Dunn mean by: "Religion and Politics are connected together?"

..................................................................................................................................

16. What is possible for a nation that understands the proper connections between religion and government, and the separate function and authority of church and state?

..................................................................................................................................

## SERMON OUTLINE SUGGESTION:

1. What is the role of true religion and the Church in society?
2. What is the role of civil government in society?
3. What are we to render to God, and what are we to render to government?
4. What are the great benefits of Christianity to citizens, rulers, and government?

# CHAPTER EIGHT

# No Establishment of Religion

T HE FOLLOWING SERMON EXCERPTS WILL HELP YOU understand the meaning of the First Amendment to the *United States Constitution*, specifically the first guarantee that, "Congress shall make no law respecting an establishment of religion." Most of the people who settled the American Colonies were Christians from various denominations. In each colony, one denomination usually became dominant. The public officials in some colonies approved the predominant denomination as the "established church." They raised taxes to pay the salaries of the established church clergy, and prevented or hindered other denominations from developing churches in their colony. This was particularly offensive to members of non-established churches (and other citizens) who were forced to pay taxes for clergy and staff salaries, administration and building costs of the state-sanctioned churches.

The movement to prohibit "an establishment of religion" was to prevent government sponsorship of a particular church denomination, because such sponsorship would exclude or discriminate against other denominations. The First Amendment provision was designed to prevent the government from interfering in church affairs, not to prevent the influence of true religion upon civil government.

Rev. Abraham Williams delivered an election day sermon before the Governor and General Court of Massachusetts in 1762. In it he commented on the need for public worship and instruction in order to preserve virtue.

> (C)ivil Societies have a right, it is their Duty, to
> encourage and maintain social public Worship of
> the Deity, and Instructions in Righteousness; for
> without social Virtues, Societies can't subsist; and
> these Virtues can't be expected, or depended on,
> without a belief in, and regard to, the Supreme Being,
> and a future World: Consequently, a religious Fear
> and Regard to God, ought to be encouraged in every
> Society, and with this View, publick social Worship
> and Instructions in social Virtues, maintained. This
> is consistent with the entire Liberty of Conscience...
> [and all should] practice that Piety and Virtue, which
> the Nature and Ends of civil Society require.[57]

During the 1600s and 1700s, Americans knew that virtue was necessary to maintain a peaceful and well-ordered civil society. To encourage people to be virtuous, they believed it was appropriate to have public worship of God and "instructions in social virtues." The civil authorities did not dictate how they were to worship God, what they were to preach, or the profession of certain doctrines. In this way, the errors made by the Established Church and civil authorities in England were not, for the most part, repeated. Even so, Americans gradually realized it was not proper to use civil authority and taxes to maintain clergy, public worship or religious instruction.

Rev. John Leland in 1791 wrote the booklet, titled, *The Rights of Conscience Inalienable, and therefore Religious Opinions not cognizable by Law. He* opposed any establishment of religion. The test of time he spoke about refers to the time between Christ's resurrection and Constantine's rule.

> Religion must have stood a time before any law
> could have been made about it; and if it did stand

---

[57] Op. cit., Abraham Williams, "An Election Sermon."

almost 300 years without law, it can still stand without it. . . . The evils of such an establishment [of religion] are many. . . . Uninspired, fallible men make their own opinions the test of orthodoxy, and use their own systems, as Rocrustus used his iron bedstead, to stretch and measure the consciences of all others by.—Where no toleration is granted to non-conformists, either ignorance and superstition prevail, or persecution rages.[58]

Rev. Leland used the pen name of Jack Nips. In a 1794 article in *The Yankee Spy*, he further explained his objections to any establishment of religion. As quoted in an earlier chapter, he believed the error was a failure to distinguish between sins and crimes. He believed that every man had a right to choose whether to worship God, and that it was wrong to make it a legal duty. It is a sin not to worship God, but it is not a crime.

When the First Amendment to the *U.S. Constitution* was ratified in 1791, it applied only to Congress and not to the States. Some States retained established religious requirements in their constitutions. Rev. Leland called for a change in the *Constitution of Massachusetts* that would respect the religious liberties of all citizens.

(The second article of the *Constitution of Massachusetts*) states "it is the right and duty of all men publicly, and at stated seasons, to worship the Supreme Being. . . ."

This duty is called a right. If every man has this right, then he has a right to judge for himself, and will hardly thank any body for turning his right into what they may call a duty. That it is the duty of men, and women too, to worship God publicly, I

---

[58] Op. cit., John Leland, "The Rights of Conscience Inalienable," pp. 9-10.

> heartily believe, but that it is the duty or wisdom of a convention or legislature to enjoin it on others, is called in question, and will be, until an instance can be given in the New Testament, that Jesus, or His apostles, gave orders therefore to the rulers of this world.

> It is the duty of men to repent and believe—to worship God in their closets and families as well as in public—and the reason why public worship is enjoined by authority, and private is omitted, is only to pave the way for some religious establishment by human law, and force taxes from the people to support avaricious priests.[59]

Rev. Leland then addressed the third article in the *Constitution of Massachusetts*. It stated that the legislature could "authorize and require the several towns" in the Commonwealth to provide for "the instruction of the public worship of God, and for the support and maintenance of public Protestant teachers, in all cases where such provision shall not be made voluntarily." Rev. Leland objected:

> If the legislature of this commonwealth have that power to institute and establish that religion, which they believe is the best in the world, by the same rule, all the legislatures of all the commonwealths, states, kingdoms and empires that are in the world, and that have been in the world, may claim the same.

> If dumb idols are called devils, and idolatry is the religion of the devil, this claim of power brings all the Gentile nations under the government of the devil. Idolatry was established by this pretended power in

---

[59] Op. cit., Jack Nips [John Leland], *The Yankee Spy.*

the Gentile nations, when the Christian religion was first sent among them; now if that establishment was right, then the apostles were wrong in separating so many thousands from the established religion. They were guilty of effecting a schism, and government was innocent of inflicting such punishment upon them and their adherents. In process of time, the religion of Christ prevailed so far that it was established in the empire of Rome; at which epoch it received a deadly wound, which gradually reduced it to superstition, fraud and ignorance . . .

I have long been of the belief that Jesus Christ instituted His worship . . . it is not left for rulers to do in these days; but, surely nothing more can be meant by it, than that the legislature shall incorporate religious societies, and oblige them to build houses for public worship. Parishes, precincts, and religious societies politically embodied, are phrases not known in the New Testament; convey ideas contrary to the spirit of the gospel, and pave the way for force and cruelty, inadmissible in Christ's kingdom, which is not of this world. . . .

Preaching by the day, by the month, by the year, annual taxes for preaching; what strange sounds these are! Not strange in these days; but such strangers in the New Testament, that they are not to be found there. How insignificant would the federal government be, if it was dependent on the laws of the states to support its officers! That government that has not force enough in it to support its officers, will soon fail; just so with the government of Jesus. The author of our religion has appointed a maintenance for His teachers; but has never told the rulers of this world to interfere in the matter. . . .

We next observe, that the legislature of Massachusetts have not power to provide for any public teachers, except they are Protestant. . . . Should one sect be pampered above others? Should not government protect all kinds of people, of every species of religion, without showing the least partiality? Has not the world had enough proofs of the impolicy and cruelty of favoring a Jew more than a Pagan, Turk, or Christian; or a Christian more than either of them? Why should a man be proscribed, or any wife disgraced, for being a Jew, a Turk, a Pagan, or a Christian of any denomination, when his talents and veracity as a civilian, entitles him to the confidence of the public? . . .

The last clause of the third article reads thus: "And every denomination of Christians, demeaning themselves peaceably, and as good subjects of the commonwealth, shall be equally under the protection of the law; and no subordination of any one sect or denomination to another, shall ever be established by law. . . ."

When the Pagans were favored by law, more than Christians, what devastation it made in the empire of Rome, [from] the first introduction of the Christian religion, until the reign of Constantine. In the first three centuries, almost two million lives were lost for conscience sake. These were men, women and children, who were as good subjects of state as any in the empire. After the change in the empire, when the Christian religion became established by law, the Pagans suffered in the same manner that the Christians had done in the ten preceding persecutions. Who can read the history of these sufferings without seeing the bad policy of establishing either of the religions in the empire?[60]

Referring to State laws that required towns to provide support for ministers, when they met for their town meeting, Rev. Leland addressed the consequences of such a procedure.

Whether these voters are spiritual, moral, or profane, they have an equal suffrage in the choice of spiritual teachers, who have, or should have, the cure of souls at heart.[61]

Rev. Leland concluded his appeal by proposing a revision to the *Constitution of Massachusetts.*

If the constitution should be revised, and anything about religion should be said in it, the following paragraph is proposed.

"To prevent the evils that have heretofore been occasioned in the world by religious establishments, and to keep up the proper distinction between religion and politics, no religious test shall ever be requested as a qualification of any officer, in any department of this government; neither shall the legislature, under this constitution, ever establish any religion by law, give any one sect a preference to another, or force any man in the commonwealth to part with his

---

[60] Ibid.
[61] Ibid.

property for the support of religious worship, or the maintenance of ministers of the gospel."[62]

As a Baptist, Rev. Leland knew the dangers of a government established religion. Some States had hindered the Baptists from forming churches. He protested the sanctioning of any denomination by the civil authority because it could lead to discrimination and persecution of other denominations. This view eventually prevailed in all of the States, though not until the nineteenth century.

The movement in America to eliminate the establishment of religion was to secure equal religious liberty for all citizens. It was to prevent the intrusion of government into religious and church matters, particularly by favoring one denomination of Christians over another. In contrast, it was not to prevent Scriptural truths and religious convictions from influencing government officials, legislators, and judges – which is precisely what Rev. Leland and all the other clergy quoted in this book were doing and did so with great success. Because they did so, they gained for themselves and for us liberty and the best – though imperfect – constitutions and governments formed by man up to that time.

## BIBLE STUDY:

1. Was it a government establishment of religion when King Nebuchadnezzar made a golden image of himself and ordered everyone in his kingdom to worship the image (i.e., worship him)? See Daniel 3:1-7.

   ...........................................................................................

2. Were Shadrach, Meshach and Abed-nego right to refuse to worship the image of the head of government, at the risk of their own lives (Daniel 3:8-30)?

   ...........................................................................................

---

[62] Ibid.

3. By their disobedience to the king, what happened to him (Daniel 3:26-30; 4:1-3)?

..................................................................................................

4. Was it a government establishment of religion when King Darius approved a law that anyone who prayed "to any god or man besides you ... shall be cast into the lions' den" (Daniel 6:4-9)?

..................................................................................................

5. Was Daniel right in continuing his life pattern of praying to God three times a day, and thus disobeying the government law at the risk of his own life (Daniel 6:10-17)?

..................................................................................................

6. By his disobedience, what happened (Daniel 6:18-28)?

..................................................................................................

7. When Jesus was before Pilate, what kingdom did He say He ruled over – a kingdom over which Pilate had no authority (John 18:28-37)?

..................................................................................................

## QUESTIONS FOR CONTEMPLATION OR DISCUSSION:

1. What was the purpose of the no "establishment of religion" clause in the First Amendment to the United States Constitution?

..................................................................................................

2. Was the purpose of that clause to prevent the influence of true religion upon civil government?

..................................................................................................

3. Between the time of Christ and Constantine, were there any government laws regulating the Christian religion?

..................................................................................................

4. What happened when Constantine made Christianity the state religion of Rome?

.......................................................................................................................................................

5. Is choosing not to worship God, or not to worship Him in a particular way, a crime?

.......................................................................................................................................................

6. What were some of Rev. Leland's concerns about government involvement in religion?

.......................................................................................................................................................

7. Did the founding generations of America intend to "prevent Scriptural truths and religious convictions from influencing government?" Why or why not?

.......................................................................................................................................................

## SERMON OUTLINE SUGGESTION:

1. Was the early Church regulated by civil government?
2. What error did Constantine make in mixing government with religion?
3. What was the purpose of the no "establishment of religion" clause in the First Amendment to the United States Constitution?
4. Did the founding generations of America intend to "prevent Scriptural truths and religious convictions from influencing government?"

# CHAPTER NINE

# Choosing Good Rulers

WHAT GUIDELINES SHOULD WE USE IN CHOOSING OUR public officials? The best public officials are those who reverently fear God and faithfully fulfill the duties of their office within the parameters of the constitution. If a public official fears God, he will respect man, the sanctity of human life, and the law. If he does not know God personally, but respects human life and the law, and does not exceed his constitutional authority, he can still be a good public official. If he does not fear God, cherish human life, keep his oath to uphold the constitution, or respect the rule of law, then he will be a tyrant. Tyrants are defined and discussed in the next chapter.

God gave Israel brief but specific guidelines for choosing their officials — guidelines that we would be wise to follow. When the LORD commanded that, "Three times in a year all your males shall appear before the LORD your God," He said,

> You shall appoint for yourself judges and officers in all your towns which the LORD your God is giving you, according to your tribes, and they shall judge the people with righteous judgment. You shall not distort justice; you shall not be partial, and you shall not take a bribe, for a bribe blinds the eyes of the wise and perverts the words of the righteous. Justice, and only justice, you shall pursue, that you may live and possess the land which the LORD your God is giving you. You shall not plant for yourself an Asherah [female idol] of any kind of tree beside the altar of the

LORD your God, which you shall make for yourself.
You shall not set up for yourself a *sacred* pillar which
the LORD your God hates (Deuteronomy 16:16-22).

Both ancient Israel and the founding generations of the United
States incorporated some of these Biblical principles in their systems
of government. In Israel, the men chose public officials from among
themselves (not foreigners, and not women) at the town, tribe (state)
and national levels. The United States has a similar representative
system, though women were also granted the right to vote through
approval of the 19ᵗʰ Amendment. The Scriptural passage above
indicates that the primary duty of public officials is to make righteous
decisions and establish justice. They were "not *to* be partial to the poor
nor defer to the great," and thus cause injustices (Leviticus 19:15).
They were never to take a bribe. This is the way our Founding Fathers
designed our system of government, though for more than a century
our government has shown partiality in many ways (e.g., graduated
tax system; social entitlements; hiring quotas by gender or ethnicity).

In 1774, Rev. Gad Hitchcock, pastor of a Congregational Church
in Pembroke, Massachusetts, gave an "Election Sermon" about good
effects of true religion on public officials.

> But that which completes the character of rulers
> and adds lustre to their other accomplishments, is
> religion. This is the best foundation of the confidence
> of the people; if they fear God, it may be expected
> they will regard man. Vice narrows the mind and
> bars the exertions of a public spirit; but religion
> dilates and strengthens the former, and gives free
> course to the operations of the latter.
>
> By religion I would be understood to intend more
> than a bare belief of the divine existence and
> perfections—The heathen world by a proper use of

their reason may attain to this, because that which may be known of God is manifest in them, for God hath shewed it unto them.

But what I intend by religion is, a belief of the truth as it is in Jesus, and a temper and conduct comfortable to it. . . . It is the wisdom of Christian states, to have Christian magistrates, and as far as may be, such as have imbibed the spirit of the gospel, and are actuated in their high station, by the principles it inspires. . . .

When a people have rulers set over them, of a religious character on the gospel plan—who own and submit to Jesus Christ as their LORD and Saviour, who are sanctified by the divine spirit and grace, and, in good measure, purified from those corrupt principles which too often work in the human heart, they have reason to expect the presence and blessing of God will be with them, and that things will go well in the state.

And on reflection, we cannot forbear the acclamation of the psalmist—happy is that people, that is in such a case!—yea, happy is that people whose God is the LORD! [Psalm 144:15] . . . The religion of rulers is a guide to their other accomplishments—it has a salutary active influence into all their measures of government, and leads them to the noblest exertions for the advancement of the common weal [well-being].

The minds of the governed are satisfied with their conduct, rejoice in their administration, and rest assured that no harm will ever happen to them, by their means, unless it be by mistake, to which all men are liable. By the blessing of the upright the city is exalted, but it is overthrown by the mouth of the wicked. [Proverbs 11:11].

. . . (F)rom a proper zeal for the divine glory, and a generous regard to their fellow men, our civil fathers will go before us in the uniform practice of pure religion, and undefiled, before God and the Father.

Under the administration of rulers of such character, we shall not rejoice merely in a civil view, but in the prosperity of our souls shall we be glad; and rejoice before God, exceedingly.[63]

Rev. Hitchcock did not advocate a religious test for public officials, but stated the wisdom of electing men of good character and strong Christian beliefs to serve in public office.

Before he takes office, every elected official must take an oath to uphold the constitution under which he will serve. This requirement is based on the principle of government by consent. The people grant their consent by electing a person to office, the authority which he receives after taking the oath. If he does not take the oath, he cannot serve in public office.

Rev. Jacob Duché gave a sermon in Philadelphia, titled, *"The Duty Of Standing Fast In Our Liberties."* He dedicated it to George Washington, who I believe was the best leader America ever had. Rev. Duché reminded Americans of the Source of all that is good, and the Source of our form of government.

Whatever of order, truth, equity and good government is to be found among the sons of men, they are solely indebted for it to this everlasting

---

[63] Op. cit., Gad Hitchcock, "An Election Sermon."

Counselor, this Prince of Peace . . . it must surely
have been this wisdom of the Father that first taught
man, by social compact, to secure to himself the
possession of those necessaries and comforts which
are so dear and valuable to his natural life.[64]

Rev. Duché believed that the idea of "social compact" was from
God, and that "true government can have no other foundation than
common consent."[65]

Faithful public servants are always mindful of their covenant with
God and the people to uphold the constitution, and are careful not
to violate it. Americans fought English rule because of the tyranny
of that government in which they had no representation. Parliament
made laws affecting the Colonies, and sought to collect taxes, even
though the colonists had no representatives in Parliament. This was
taxation without representation.

Our Founding Fathers based their new system of government
upon consent of the people. The American people granted their
consent by sending representatives to the Continental Congresses
of 1774, 1775 and 1776, to discuss common concerns about the
abuses of power by Great Britain. They granted their consent
through their representatives to declare independence, and to form
a new government. When the first form of national government
(*Articles of Confederation*) failed, the States sent representatives to a
Constitutional Convention to reform it. Instead of reforming the old
one, they created an entirely new form of government, proposed as the
*United States Constitution*. The Convention sent the new *Constitution*
to the American people for their approval. Once nine (of the original
13) States approved it, it became our new form of government. Today,
we grant our consent by electing representatives and requiring them
to take an oath to uphold the *Constitution*.

---

[64] Op. cit., Jacob Duché, "Duty of Standing Fast in Our Liberties," p. 82.
[65] Ibid., pp. 81-82.

Elected officials should restrict the use of their power to lawful limits. They should read the constitution to ensure they have the authority to do something before they do it, and not depend upon judges and other officials to determine constitutionality. However, if a court does rule on the constitutionality of a law or government program, officials are obligated to abide by that ruling. However, if an official believes a ruling is unconstitutional, he has no obligation to uphold it, since he retains an independent responsibility to uphold the constitution within his sphere of authority. Thus, if a court makes a bad decision, it should only affect the parties involved in the case, and not change the laws.

In 1779, Dr. Stillman spoke to the public officials of Massachusetts Bay prior to the convention to form a state constitution. Through his sermon, titled, *"The Duty of Magistrates,"* he identified ways a public official — as an individual, as head of his family, and as a magistrate — can encourage true religion and what is good in society.

> A faithful ruler will consider himself as a trustee of the public, and that he is accountable both to God and to the people for his behavior in his office.
>
> *"He who ruleth over men,"* says David, *"must be just, ruling in the fear of God"* [2 Samuel 23:3] . . . that all those who united in [electing him] . . . may uninterruptedly enjoy that *equal liberty*, for the security of which they entered into a state of civil society. . . . (T)here are many ways in which the civil magistrate may encourage religion, in a perfect agreement with the nature of the kingdom of Christ, and the rights of conscience.
>
> As a *man*, he is *personally* interested in it. His everlasting salvation is at stake. Therefore, he should search the Scriptures for himself, and follow

them wherever they lead him. This right he hath in common with every other citizen. As the *head of a family*, he should act as a priest in his own house, by endeavoring to bring up his children in the nurture and admonition of the LORD. As a *magistrate*, he should be as a nursing father to the church of Christ, by protecting all the peaceable members of it from injury on account of religion; and by securing to them the uninterrupted enjoyment of equal religious liberty. The authority by which he acts he derives alike from *all the people*; consequently he should exercise that authority *equally* for the benefit of *all*, without any respect to their different religious principles. They have an undoubted right to demand it.[66]

True religion has a good effect on leaders, as it makes them mindful of their duties to God, their families, and the people. The religious activities mentioned above are not contrary to their public duties. None of the ways suggested to encourage true religion and good behavior imposes on the religious or civil liberties of other citizens who do not share the same beliefs. Moreover, a public official has a duty to ensure that every citizen may enjoy "equal religious liberty."

Good public officials have a good effect on society because they preserve both the liberties of the people and the government by upholding the constitution and laws of the land. Those who govern *"in the fear of God,"* and who have strong moral convictions based on true religion, will be the best public leaders and servants. They will most likely keep their oath of office, not abuse the power of that office, protect human life, and respect the rule of law.

---

[66] Op. cit., Samuel Stillman, "The Duty of Magistrates," pp. 280-281.

# Important Questions for Choosing Officials:

Sadly, today it seems to be popular to ridicule, mock, and rebel against Christian officials, and chase or coerce them out of office, instead of praising them for their faithful service. Let's change that by encouraging those who serve in public office, and by replacing those who are abusing or going beyond the powers entrusted to them.

Here are some important questions to ask when choosing candidates for public office. These guidelines are based on the Scriptures, and the principles articulated by Dr. Stillman, Rev. Leland and others. Before voting for a candidate, try to answer the following questions:

- Does he reverently fear God? Does he recognize accountability to God?
- Does he recognize that *all* men are created equal, and respect all citizens, regardless of their religious beliefs, male or female, age, color, or economic status?
- Does he recognize which rights are unalienable, and is he committed to preserving those rights (e.g., life, freedom of religion, rights of conscience, property)?
- Does he believe civil government should not interfere in matters of religion, conscience, the mind, and education?
- Does he believe the purpose of civil government is to encourage good behavior and punish evil behavior?
- Does he believe that the first purpose of civil government is to protect human life (including preborn and newly born children), and always punish those who deliberately take another's life?
- If elected, will he faithfully keep his oath to uphold the constitution by fulfilling his duties and not exceeding the bounds of his authority?

## Why did the Lᴏʀᴅ God choose only men to bear the sword?

God clearly gave men the duties of protecting and defending, of civil government and executing lawful law, of exercising the power of the sword, of force and the military. Why did the Lᴏʀᴅ God deliberately choose only men for these purposes, and promise to bless and protect their nation if they followed His instructions (Exodus 34:23-24; Deuteronomy 16:16-20)? This does not mean that women cannot serve in administrative and supportive roles in civil government. For decades now we have been experiencing a historical anomaly with so many women in government as officials, legislators, judges, policemen and military. Therefore, this is a very important question since our present generations have forgotten and rejected these Biblical commands, principles, instructions and promises.

Let's first look at the original order of God. When God created Man (mankind), He named them 'âdam [Hebrew 120],[67] which includes "male and female" (Genesis 1:26-27). Our first identity is equality before God and each other! But then God made distinctions.

In Genesis 1:27, the first Hebrew word for "male" is zâkâr [H2145], which means *"remembered, a male, memorial to parents."* This word is derived from zâkar [H2142], meaning *"to mark, to remember, to recollect, to bring to mind, to record; pricking, piercing, penetrating, infixing; memory; to keep, to preserve*; by implication, to be male; to recollect, bring to mind."[68] A pattern in Scripture is that we are given an overview first, and then a second account with more detail. God revealed in Genesis 1 that He created Man "in the image of God," as "male and female." Then He revealed in Genesis 2 that He made Man as male first, which corresponds to the order of the Trinity. God the Father is the head, but Jesus and the Holy Spirit are equal members of the Godhead. When God created Adam first, He gave

---

[67] From www.BlueLetterBible.org, which includes Strong's Definitions, Brown-Driver-Briggs Lexicon, and Gesenius' Hebrew-Chaldee Lexicon.
[68] Ibid.

him certain commands to obey, and the responsibility to remember and communicate those commands to his wife and family when God created them. Adam was given primary responsibility to represent Father God, remember and impart the Word of God, and protect his wife and family spiritually and physically.

When God created Man, He said, "Let Us make man in Our image, according to Our likeness" (Genesis 1:26). Rev. Bill Cook shared with me his realization that this was the only instance in the Creation narrative that God spoke of "Us." In every other instance, He said, "let there be . . . ." In Genesis 2 we are given more detail about the order of creation. After God made Man as male first, and placed him in the Garden of Eden, He said, "It is not good for the man to be alone; I will make him a helper suitable (corresponding) for him" (Genesis 2:18). Why? Because, as Rev. Cook explained, it was not good that man remain a unary being, for as such he was incapable of fully reflecting the triune nature of God. It was necessary to make Eve, because before Eve existed Adam was not yet an "us." When God made Eve, He did not fashion her out of dust of the Earth. She was made out of Adam. After God fashioned Eve from Adam's "rib" (side), Adam was still Adam, but now they were an "us." Together they could reflect the nature of God and fulfill the mandate to "Be fruitful and multiply, and fill the earth, and subdue it" (Genesis 1:28).

In Genesis 1:27, the first Hebrew word for "female" is neqêbâh [H5347], meaning *a woman, a female.* This word is derived from nâqab [H5344], meaning *"to puncture, to bore (a hole); to separate, to distinguish"*; and means to be open to receive.[69] God created a woman to be open to receive both spiritual and natural seed from her husband, and to nurture and give life to those seeds. But being open to receive, she also has a natural vulnerability to deception. The Fall of mankind occurred when Eve was deceived and tempted by the serpent, and Adam stayed silent, not remembering and

---

[69] Ibid.

proclaiming the Word of God, and thus failing to protect his wife from deception. Immediately after that sin, God came directly to Adam, first holding him accountable (Genesis 3:1-11). From this created order of God, and the nature of how He created male and female, He chose men to protect women and children, their cities and nation, and to directly exercise the forceful powers of civil government, military and police (Genesis 14:14-16; Exodus 18:13-26; Numbers 1:1-46).

A profound difference was discovered between the brains of males and females. Dr. James C. Dobson, in his book *Bringing Up Boys*, described what happens in the womb during pregnancy if the baby is a boy (with the male Y chromosome):

> (A)t six or seven weeks after conception . . . a dramatic spiking of testosterone occurs . . . It begins masculinizing their tiny bodies and transforming them into boys. In a real sense, this 'hormonal bath', as it is sometimes called, actually damages the walnut-shaped brain and alters its structure in many ways. Even its color changes. The corpus callosum, which is the rope of nerve fibers that connects the two hemispheres, is made less sufficient. That limits the number of electrical transmissions that can flow from one side of the brain to the other, which will have lifelong implications. Later, a man will have to think longer about what he believes—especially about something with an emotional component. He may never fully comprehend it. A woman, on the other hand, will typically be able to access her prior experience from both hemispheres and discern almost instantly how she feels about it."[70]

---

[70] James C. Dobson, <u>Bringing Up Boys</u> (Wheaton, IL: Tyndale House Publishers, 2001), p. 19-20.

The effect for males is the propensity and ability to compartmentalize.[71] This gives them the capacity to do certain things without destroying themselves or others emotionally and physically. A man is designed to be able to stand for God and His Word in the face of opposition, as God's first representative, as an act of love for God and for those whom he is protecting and to whom he is speaking. A man is designed to be able to obey God even when he is tempted by others to not obey, when he would rather say nothing or yield to his wife or someone else. A man can serve as a policeman or soldier, and perform his duties or go to war – and be traumatized – but be able to return home and love his wife and children, blocking out those memories, at least partially, until he has time and opportunity to process them. For a woman to experience the same is far more traumatic and deeply damaging to her soul and feminine nature. As I have observed women serving in these capacities, they seem to gradually lose their femininity, their tender and nurturing nature, and become harder and increasingly like men.

These are important considerations in choosing public rulers – whether government leaders, legislators or judges – and when deciding whether to allow women to be policemen or serve in combat positions in the military. God created women to give and nurture life. When a woman intentionally takes a life, or is trained to take life, or must exercise civil or military force, it is contrary and destructive to her nature.

People are free to choose whomever they want to serve in government and military, but cannot control the consequences of those choices. Furthermore, every citizen has a duty to respect and honor the office regardless of who was entrusted with that authority (though a citizen is not obligated to obey a command or law that is contrary to the Law of God). If leaders and citizens bring their choices

---

[71] An excellent book describing this reality, with some humor, is Men Are Like Waffles, Women Are Like Spaghetti, by Bill and Pam Farrel (Harvest House Publishers, 2017).

and decisions in conformity with the order given by God, then they will have His blessing, peace and protection; but if not, they will not, and instead will have disorder, divisions, strife, conflicts and attacks.

Here are some final thoughts from Rev. Bill Cook and me. Rev. Cook addressed a critical related issue of our time that is destroying men, women and our society. He said that "by tolerating sodomy and legitimizing same-sex 'marriage,' our people and nations are undermining our God-given mission to fulfill the dominion mandate, thus ensuring our own demise. That is why Sodom and Gomorrah were destroyed." We should heed the warning! He continued, "sodomy and the shedding of innocent blood are utter rebellion against the design and purpose of God in making Man, and against the Law of Nature. That is why in early America, sodomy was prosecuted as a capital crime, the punishment for which was public execution."[72]

That punishment may seem excessively cruel because we do not realize the extreme destructive power of sin. Before the LORD brought His people into the land He promised to give them, He gave them His Law and warned them not to follow in the same sins and abominations of the pagan nations in that land. God also warned them to purge evil from their midst, from among yourselves. In 40 years of public policy related to nations, I have observed that any sin that is allowed to flourish will increase unabated, take over, and destroy all that is good in a community or nation.

I am persuaded that the two most important factors to restoring our families, communities, and nations are for (1) men to regain their true identity and rise up and fulfill their God-given responsibilities – with women, the Church, and society supporting them; and (2) for clergy and the whole Church to arise and be light, salt, and "the pillar and support of the Truth" (1 Timothy 3:15).

---

[72] "The Cry of Sodom Enquired Into, Upon Occasion of the Arraignment and Condemnation of Benjamin Goad, for His Prodigious Villany," an Execution Sermon preached by Rev. Samuel Danforth, 1674; https://digitalcommons.unl.edu/cgi/viewcontent.cgi?article=1024&context=zeaamericanstudies.

## Bible study:

1.  Who did God choose, or say to choose, for civil government leadership and military, to represent and protect the people (Exodus 3:1-10; 34:23-24; Numbers 1:1-46; Deuteronomy 16:16-20; 31:14-23; Joshua 1:1-9; Judges 3:9, 15; 6:11-14; 1 Samuel 9:17; 13:8-14; 16:1-13)?

    ..................................................................................................

2.  What are the characteristics of the men God said to choose for civil rulers, or instructions He gave regarding their duties (Exodus 18:21, 25; 23:6-8; Leviticus 19:15; Deuteronomy 1:15-18; 16:18-20; 2 Samuel 23:1-5)?

    ..................................................................................................

3.  Joseph was repeatedly promoted, and became Prime Minister of Egypt. How would you describe his character (Genesis 39 – 41)?

    ..................................................................................................

4.  Daniel was one of the top three government leaders under King Darius. How is His character described (Daniel 6:4)?

    ..................................................................................................

5.  What had to occur before a chosen king or ruler could take office (2 Samuel 5:1-4)?

    ..................................................................................................

6.  What are some of the results from "the blessing of the upright," including rulers that are righteous (Proverbs 11:11)?

    ..................................................................................................

7.  Who are the most blessed people and nation on earth (Psalm 144:15)?

    ..................................................................................................

8.  How did God uniquely make males?

    ..................................................................................................

9. How did God uniquely make females?

......................................................................................................

10. Why did God choose men for civil government, police and military, where force – the power of the sword – must be exercised?

......................................................................................................

## QUESTIONS FOR CONTEMPLATION OR DISCUSSION:

1. Why did Rev. Hitchcock say true religion has a profoundly good effect upon rulers?

......................................................................................................

2. What must an elected official, legislator or judge, or any of their staff, do before they can exercise the authority and power of that office, or serve in a supportive manner (e.g., as I did to serve on Congressional staff)?

......................................................................................................

3. To what is an elected official required to restrict the exercise of the powers entrusted to him?

......................................................................................................

4. Over what areas did Dr. Stillman say a good ruler could live out his Christian faith and have noble influence?

......................................................................................................

5. What good effects can true religion have on leaders and rulers?

......................................................................................................

6. Who are potentially the best leaders and rulers?

......................................................................................................

7. Review, consider and discuss the Important Questions for Choosing Officials.

......................................................................................................

## SERMON OUTLINE SUGGESTION:

1. What responsibilities did God give uniquely to men in society?
2. What character qualities did God say we should require of our leaders and candidates for public office?
3. What important questions should we ask when choosing candidates for office?
4. How did God make male and female differently for their mutual benefit, and how should this impact who we choose for public office?
5. How would our community and nation be different and better if men regained their true identity and fully embraced their God-given responsibilities?

# CHAPTER TEN

# Obey Good Rulers, Resist Tyrants Respectfully & Firmly

THE PREVIOUS CHAPTER DESCRIBED GOOD PUBLIC LEADERS and officials, and guidelines for choosing them. Let us now examine the duties of citizens in relation to their leaders. The Word of God proclaims in Romans 13:1-5:

> Let every person be in subjection to the governing authorities. For there is no authority except from God, and those which exist are established by God. Therefore he who resists authority has opposed the ordinance of God; and they who have opposed will receive condemnation upon themselves. For rulers are not a cause of fear for good behavior, but for evil. Do you want to have no fear of authority? Do what is good, and you will have praise from the same; for it is a minister of God to you for good. But if you do what is evil, be afraid; for it does not bear the sword for nothing; for it is a minister of God, an avenger who brings wrath upon the one who practices evil.... (I) t is necessary to be in subjection, not only because of wrath, but also for conscience' sake.

Many people read this passage and assume that to be in proper subjection to God, they must do everything the governing authorities tell them to do, even if wrong or evil, but that is not what Scripture says. Romans 13 becomes clear when we understand the meaning of "authorities" or "powers". The Greek word is "exousias," meaning "privilege, force, capacity, competency, mastery or (delegated) influence," and is translated as "magistrate, authority, jurisdiction, power, right or strength." Exousia comes from the word, "exesti," which means, "it is right" or "it is lawful."[73] Therefore, a government official is functioning as a "minister of God" when he exercises the authority entrusted to him in a right and lawful manner, encouraging good and punishing those who do evil. Obedience to such officials is a solemn Christian duty. The clergy cited later in this chapter address this duty of obedience, as well as when it is right to resist or not obey.

There are several conclusions I draw from Romans 13 regarding a citizen's duty to public officials:

- God alone has absolute authority;
- All human authorities derive their lawful and just authority from God;
- All lawful governing authorities are "established by God," accountable to Him, and are to remain within His prescribed purpose for government;
- God designed civil government to encourage good and punish evil behavior, to "bear the sword" as "an avenger who brings wrath upon the one who practices evil";
- Citizens have a duty to God to "be in subjection" to their public officials;
- If the civil government becomes "a cause for fear for good behavior, but [not] for evil," it has ceased to fulfill its God-given purpose, acting contrary to His will;
- The same command that compels citizens to obey their public officials, requires citizens to resist them when they are acting as tyrants.

---

[73] Strong's Exhaustive Concordance of the Bible, with Greek and Hebrew Dictionary (Nashville, TN: Crusade Bible Publishers, Inc.). And www.BlueLetterBible.org.

What are tyrants? They are government legislators, officials, judges, police, military, or others who misuse their office and exceed the authority granted them, or who act against the revealed will and Law of God. *Webster's 1828 Dictionary* defines a "tyrant" by listing ways they abuse their power.

> A monarch or other ruler or master, who uses power to oppress his subjects; a person who exercises unlawful authority, or lawful authority in an unlawful manner; one who by taxation, injustice or cruel punishment, or the demand for unreasonable services, imposes burdens and hardships on those under his control, which law and humanity do not authorize, or which the purposes of government do not require.[74]

In 1750, Dr. Jonathan Mayhew gave a sermon in Boston titled, *A Discourse Concerning Unlimited Submission and Non-Resistance to the Higher Powers*. He was one of the most well-known and respected preachers of his time.

> For magistracy and government being . . . the ordinance and appointment of God, it follows, that to resist magistrates in the execution of their offices, is really to resist the will and ordinance of God Himself; and they who resist will accordingly be punished by God for this sin, in common with others. . . . If they turn tyrants, and become the common oppressors of those whose welfare they ought to regard with paternal affection . . . whether we are obliged to yield . . . absolute submission to our prince, or whether disobedience and resistance may not be justifiable in some cases, notwithstanding

---

[74] Op. cit., Noah Webster, <u>An American Dictionary</u>, s.v. "tyrant."

anything in the passage before us, is an inquiry in which we all are concerned. . . .

(T)here does not seem to be any necessity of supposing that an absolute, unlimited obedience, whether active or passive, is here enjoined. . . .

Children are commanded to obey their parents, and servants their masters, in as absolute and unlimited terms as subjects are here commanded to obey their civil rulers. . . . But who supposes that the apostle ever intended to teach that children, servants, and wives, should, in all cases whatever, obey their parents, masters, and husbands respectively, never making any opposition to their will, even although they should require them to break the commandments of God, or should causelessly make an attempt upon their lives? No one puts such a sense upon these expressions, however absolute and unlimited. . . .

It is obvious . . . that the civil rulers whom the apostle here speaks of, and obedience to whom he presses upon Christians as a duty, are good rulers, such as are, in the exercise of their office and power, benefactors to society. Such they are described throughout this passage. Thus, it is said that they are not a terror to good works, but to the evil; that they are God's ministers for good. . . . If rulers are a terror to good works, and not to the evil; if they are not ministers for good to society, but for evil and distress, by violence and oppression; if they execute wrath upon sober, peaceable persons, who do their duty as members of society . . . if, instead of attending continually upon the good work of advancing the public welfare, they attend continually upon the gratification of their own lust and pride and ambition, to the destruction of the public welfare;—if this be the case, it is plain that the apostle's argument for submission does not reach them; they are not the same, but different persons from those whom he characterizes, and who must be obeyed, according to his reasoning. . . .

"Let every soul be subject unto the higher powers; for there is no power but of God: the powers that be are ordained of God" (Romans 13:1). . . . (T)hose who resist a reasonable and just authority, which is agreeable to the will of God, do really resist the will of God Himself, and will, therefore, be punished by Him. But how does this prove that those who resist a lawless, unreasonable power, which is contrary to the will of God, do therein resist the will and ordinance of God? Is resisting those who resist God's will the same thing with resisting God? . . .

"But if thou do that which is evil, be afraid: for he is the minister of God, a revenger, to execute wrath upon him that doth evil" (Romans 13:4). Here the apostle argues, from the nature and end of magistracy, that such as did evil, and such only, had reason to be afraid of the higher powers; it being part of their office to punish evil-doers, no less than to defend and encourage such as do well. But if magistrates are unrighteous,—if they are respecters of persons,—if they are partial in their administration of justice,—then those who do well have as much reason to be afraid as those that do evil: there can be no safety for the good, nor any peculiar ground of terror to the

unruly and injurious; so that, in this case, the main
end of civil government will be frustrated.[75]

Dr. Mayhew said that God alone had absolute authority, that He
does not govern arbitrarily, and that resistance to arbitrary, oppressive
human rulers was proper before God. No one has a right to command
another to do what is wrong. God has given every creature in nature
the means of self-defense, and every person and nation have a right
to act in self-defense.

Dr. Mayhew had a different interpretation of Romans 13 than is
common today. He, and most of his contemporaries, understood it
to be *prescriptive*; that is, to give us God's instructions for the proper
foundation and purpose of civil government. They knew it was *not
descriptive* of most governments. Otherwise, first-century Christians
would not have, at the cost of their lives, refused to obey the command
to renounce Christ and worship Caesar. Also, the Americans would
not have resisted the tyranny of England, and we would not be a
free people. Although Dr. Mayhew gave this sermon 25 years before
the War for Independence, he did help prepare Americans for
independence.

Rev. Samuel West preached one of the finest sermons of the
century on 29 May 1776, before the Council and the House of
Representatives of the Colony of Massachusetts-Bay, a few weeks prior
to the signing of the *Declaration of Independence*. Rev. West explained
that submission to good government and resistance to tyranny have
the same foundation, and that the perfect exercise of liberty even in a
state of nature is always consistent with the will of God.

> We find our blessed Saviour directing the Jews to
> render to Caesar the things that were Caesar's; and
> the apostles and first preachers of the gospel not
> only exhibited a good example of subjection to the

---

[75] Op. cit., Jonathan Mayhew, "Unlimited Submission," pp. 57, 63-66, 70-71, 74-76.

magistrate . . . but they also . . . strongly enjoined upon Christians the duty of submission to that government under which Providence had placed them. . . .

In order, therefore, that we may form a right judgment of the duty enjoined in our text, I shall consider the nature and design of civil government, and shall show that the same principles which oblige us to submit to government do equally oblige us to resist tyranny; or that tyranny and magistracy are so opposed to each other that where the one begins the other ends. . . .

That we may understand the nature and design of civil government, and discover the foundation of the magistrate's authority to command, and the duty of subjects to obey, it is necessary to . . . consider what "state all men are naturally in . . . (as Mr. Locke observes) a state of perfect freedom to order all their actions, and dispose of their possessions and persons as they think fit, within the bounds of the laws of nature, without asking leave or depending upon the will of any man." It is a state wherein all are equal,— no one having a right to control another, or oppose him in what he does, unless it be in his own defence, or in the defence of those that, being injured, stand in need of his assistance. . . .

(A) state of nature, though it be a state of perfect freedom, yet is very far from a state of licentiousness. The law of nature gives men no right to do anything that is immoral, or contrary to the will of God, and injurious to their fellow-creatures; for a state of nature is properly a state of law and government, even a government founded upon the unchangeable nature of the Deity, and the law resulting from the eternal fitness of things. Sooner shall heaven and earth pass away, and the whole frame of nature be dissolved, than any part even the smallest iota, of this law shall ever be abrogated; it is unchangeable as the Deity Himself....

It is our duty to endeavor always to promote the general good; to do all as we would be willing to be done by were we in their circumstances; to do justly, to love mercy, and to walk humbly before God. [Micah 6:8] These are some of the laws of nature which every man in the world is bound to observe, and which whoever violates exposes himself to the resentment of mankind, the lashes of his own conscience, and the judgment of Heaven. This plainly shows that the highest state of liberty subjects us to the law of nature and the government of God. The most perfect freedom consists in obeying the dictates of right reason, and submitting to natural law. When a man goes beyond or contrary to the law of nature and reason, he becomes the slave of base passions and vile lusts; he introduces confusion and disorder into society, and brings misery and destruction upon himself. . . . Hence we conclude that where licentiousness begins, liberty ends....

As our duty of obedience to the magistrate is founded upon our obligation to promote the general good, our readiness to obey lawful authority will always arise in proportion to the love and regard that we have for the welfare of the public; and the same love and regard for the public will inspire us with as strong a zeal to oppose tyranny as we have to obey magistracy....

Unlimited submission and obedience is due to none but God alone. He has an absolute right to command; He alone has an uncontrollable sovereignty over us, because He alone is unchangeably good....

If magistrates are ministers of God only because the law of God and reason points out the necessity of such an institution for the good of mankind, it follows, that whenever they pursue measures directly destructive of the public good they cease being God's ministers, they forfeit their right to obedience from the subject . . . and the community is under the strongest obligation of duty, both to God and to its own members, to resist and oppose them, which will be so far from resisting the ordinance of God that it will be strictly obeying His commands....

The liberty of the subject is also clearly asserted, viz., that subjects are to be allowed to do everything that is in itself just and right, and are only to be restrained from being guilty of wrong actions. It is also strongly implied, that when rulers become oppressive to the subjects and injurious to the state, their authority, their respect, their maintenance, and the duty of submitting to them, must immediately cease; they are then to be considered as the ministers of Satan, and, as such, it becomes our indispensable duty to resist and oppose them.[76]

---

[76] Op. cit., Samuel West, "A Sermon Preached before the Honorable Council, and the Honorable House of Representatives," pp. 269-271, 273, 282-284, 296.

America is free because our forefathers understood that they had a solemn duty before God to obey magistrates and resist tyrants. They were convinced it was right for them to resist the British, and that their cause was just. If they had been unwilling to resist the tyranny of Great Britain, they would not have gained freedom for themselves and for us. How should we be following their example today?

## BIBLE STUDY:

1.  What does the word "authorities" or "powers" mean in Romans 13:1-3?

    ...................................................................................................................................

2.  What is the purpose of civil government (Genesis 9:5-6; Romans 13:1-5)?

    ...................................................................................................................................

3.  Who in government are "ministers of God" and who are not (Romans 13:3-4)?

    ...................................................................................................................................

4.  Does Scripture require absolute obedience to government? Why or why not?

    ...................................................................................................................................

5.  What other observations do you conclude from Romans 13:1-5?

    ...................................................................................................................................

## QUESTIONS FOR CONTEMPLATION OR DISCUSSION:

1.  In chapter 2, Dr. Mayhew observed: "God Himself does not govern in an absolutely arbitrary and despotic manner." In this chapter, what did Dr. Mayhew observe about wives in relationship to their husbands, children in relation to their parents, servants in relation to their masters, and citizens

in relation to their government? Does God require absolute obedience to any of these human authorities? Why or why not?

.................................................................................................................

2. Where does government authority come from?

.................................................................................................................

3. What is the difference between a good magistrate (in government) and a tyrant?

.................................................................................................................

4. Obedience to lawful authority is obedience to ............................ .

5. Resistance to tyranny, if for the right reasons and in the right manner before God, can also be obedience to ......................, and can restore lawful government authority.

6. Rev. West said that "tyranny and magistracy are so opposed to each other that ... .........................................................................................."

7. Rev. West also rightly said that "Unlimited submission and obedience is due to" who alone?

.................................................................................................................

Why?

.................................................................................................................

## SERMON OUTLINE SUGGESTION:

1. What is the purpose of civil government?
2. What truths about civil government do we find in Romans 13:1-5.
3. Who in government are "ministers of God" and who are tyrants?
4. What are our duties before God, and what are expected results of obedience?

# CHAPTER ELEVEN

# The Truth About the American Revolution

A T LEAST A QUARTER CENTURY BEFORE THE AMERICAN Revolution, clergy were diligently preparing the people for independence – not for war – by teaching them truths about the sovereignty of God, liberty, self-government, and civil government. Through their instruction, the people understood lawful authority and government, and how it differed from tyranny. They knew the importance of respecting lawful authority, resisting tyranny, and taking bold actions to preserve their religious and civil liberties, and create a free government. It was the Spirit of God working through the unbridled clergy and Church that set Americans free before the war ever began.

In 1750, Dr. Jonathan Mayhew, in his sermon titled, *A Discourse Concerning Unlimited Submission and Non-Resistance to the Higher Powers*, revealed a clear understanding of history, and prophetic insight of America's future. On the basis of Romans 13:1-8, he challenged the "divine right of kings, and the doctrine of non-resistance."

> The hereditary, indefeasible, divine right of kings, and the doctrine of non-resistance, which is built upon the supposition of such a right, are ... absurd ... [and are] notions [which] are fetched neither from divine revelation nor human reason.[77]

---

[77] Op. cit., Jonathan Mayhew, "Unlimited Submission," pp. 84, 88-89, 92, 94-95.

In previous chapters, Dr. Mayhew observed that "God Himself does not govern in an absolutely arbitrary and despotic manner," and compared the obedience due to parents and masters (employers) with that due to civil authorities. He believed that people who suffer under "an absolutely arbitrary and despotic" government have the duty to remove the oppressors.

> For a nation thus abused to arise unanimously and resist their prince, even to the dethroning him, is not criminal, but a reasonable way of vindicating their liberties and just rights: it is making use of the means, and the only means, which God has put into their power for mutual and self defence. And it would be highly criminal in them not to make use of this means.[78]

The American Colonies, 26 years later, rejected the divine right of kings, removed themselves out from under the King of England's power, and formed constitutional governments to preserve their "liberties and just rights." Ironically, England's own history provided an example. Dr. Mayhew's sermon marked the 100th anniversary of the overthrow of King Charles. After summarizing the many abuses of power committed by Charles against his own people—including civil and religious leaders—he asked the following questions:

> For what reason, then, was the resistance to King Charles made? . . . (I)t was on account of the tyranny and oppression of his reign. . . .
>
> But by whom was this resistance made? Not by a private junto, not by a small seditious party, not by a few desperadoes, who to mend their fortunes would

---

[78] Ibid.

embroil the state; but by the Lords and Commons of England. It was they that almost unanimously opposed the king's measures for overturning the constitution, and changing that free and happy government into a wretched, absolute monarchy. It was they that—when the king was about levying forces against his subjects in order to make himself absolute—commissioned officers, and raised an army to defend themselves and the public; and it was they that maintained the war against him all along, till he was made a prisoner. . . .

The nation had been patient under the oppressions of the crown, even to long-suffering, for a course of many years, and there was no rational hope of redress in any other way. Resistance was absolutely necessary, in order to preserve the nation from slavery, misery, and ruin. And who so proper to make this resistance as the Lords and Commons,—the whole representative body of the people,—guardians of the public welfare; and each which was, in point of legislation, vested with an equal, coordinate power with that of the crown?[79]

There are parallels between England's response to King Charles and the Americans' response to King George III. Both began with a long period of appeals, and ended in armed defense once all possibility of appeal was exhausted and the king had ordered his army to attack the people. In each case, lawfully elected representatives of the people, who had their support, led the resistance. Good magistrates acted responsibly to protect the lives, liberty, and property of the people; and to preserve a constitutional form of government.

---

[79] Ibid.

In America, representatives of the Colonies began appealing to the King of England and to Parliament in 1763. They continued their appeals for twelve years. But when British forces attacked the Colonists, they appealed to God for assistance, and through their elected representatives raised up an army to defend themselves.

In December 1774, Rev. William Gordon, who had great influence in the Colonies, preached at the Boston Lecture. He knew the conflict with Great Britain was imminent. Nevertheless, he believed God would preserve this land as a sanctuary for those fleeing religious and civil oppression.

> And how will the surviving inhabitants and their posterity, together with refugees who have fled from oppression and hardships, whether civil or sacred, to our American sanctuary, daily give thanks to the Sovereign of the universe that this general asylum was not consumed! How oft will they, with raptures . . . bless that God who owned the goodness of it, and at length crowned it with success! Hallelujah. The LORD God omnipotent reigneth.[80]

Rev. Gordon was confident that God would give America victory five months before the British fired the first shots in Lexington. Let us "daily give thanks to the Sovereign of the universe," who gave us liberty by crowning the Colonists efforts with success. Our liberty is the gift of God, but it was purchased by the blood of Jesus Christ (who died that all men might be free), and the blood of thousands of Americans.

Rev. Elisha Rich preached *A Sermon On Ecclesiastical Liberty* in 1775. Although Americans were confident that their cause was just, Rev. Rich was concerned that injustices in the Colonies could subvert the opportunity for liberty. The misuse of civil power in

---

[80] Op. cit., William Gordon, "A Discourse Preached on . . . the day recommended by the Provincial Congress," pp. 225-226.

matters of religion alarmed him, and he did not believe we would gain our freedom if our own government continued such abuses. In the preface, he said,

> The sound of Liberty being so frequently heard, through our American-Colonies, hath emboldened many of her Sons to vindicate her cause, against the cruel hand of oppression. . . .

> I was in hopes, since people were so warm for civil liberty, that they would not be so glaringly inconsistent as to be religious tyrants. I hoped we should have no more cause to oppose religious oppression: But hearing of a shocking instance of this kind of oppression (I might justly call it robbery) . . . in . . . Massachusetts-Bay, acted by pretended Patriots for liberty, who, as I was informed forceably took the substance of two men, who by conviction of their conscience, differed from them to support their way of worship, and as a number of people arose to relieve the oppressed; two men were taken by authority, and bound like criminals & carried in a cart, to Cambridge GOAL and there confined. I thought it was high time for babes to break their silence, and shew their resentment, against the exercise of civil power, in ecclesiastical matters, which has been the cause of much tumult and disorders . . . and I think, we may for ever bid farewell to peace, while such religious tyranny live among us. . . .[81]

Rev. Jacob Duché preached on *The Duty Of Standing Fast In Our Liberties*, on 7 July 1775. The War for Independence had begun less than three months earlier, on 19 April 1775, when the British fired on

---

[81] Op. cit., Elisha Rich, "A Sermon on Ecclesiastical Liberty," pp. ii-iv.

Americans in Lexington, Massachusetts. Rev. Duché dedicated the sermon to General George Washington, to encourage him and the Americans.

> Inasmuch, therefore, as this solemn delegation was intended for the good of the whole; inasmuch as all rulers are in fact the servants of the public, and appointed for no other purpose than to be "a terror to evil-doers, and a praise to them that do well" [Romans 13:3-4]; whenever this divine order is inverted, whenever these rulers abuse their sacred trust, by unrighteous attempts to injure, oppress, and enslave those very persons, from whom alone, under God, their power is derived—does not humanity, does not reason, does not Scripture, call upon the man, the citizen, the Christian of such a community, to "stand fast in that liberty wherewith Christ (in their very birth, as well as by succeeding appointments of His Providence) hath made them free!"[82] [Galatians 5:1]

About two weeks later, Rev. David Jones (1736-1820) preached a sermon titled, a *Defensive War In A Just Cause Sinless*. It was the Day of the Continental Fast; the American people were praying to God for His intervention, protection, guidance, and resolution of the armed conflict. He encouraged them that their cause was just, because a defensive war was sinless before God. The Americans did not initiate hostilities, did not separate from England until more than a year later, and attempted reconciliation with England. America was not the aggressor, but refused to give up her freedom.

---

[82] Op. cit., Jacob Duché, "Duty of Standing Fast in Our Liberties," p. 82.

"And I looked and rose up, and said unto the nobles, and to the rulers, and to the rest of the people, 'Be not ye afraid of them: Remember the LORD, which is great and terrible, and fight for your brethren, your sons and your daughters, your wives and your houses'" (Nehemiah 4:14).

ISRAEL, when first planted in the land of Canaan, were a brave, heroic and virtuous people, being firmly attached to the true worship of God. They were both formidable and invincible: when their armies went forth to battle, thousands and tens of thousands fell before them: thus being clothed with the majesty of virtue and true religion, a panic seized the hearts of all their enemies around them. But when vice and immorality became prevalent; when they forsook and rebelled against their God, they lost their martial spirit, and were soon enslaved by the king of Babylon.[83]

---

[83] David Jones, A.M. (1736-1820), "Defensive War In a Just Cause Sinless, a Sermon preached on the Continental Fast Day," July 20, 1775, in Tredyffryn, Chester County, Pennsylvania. Reprinted in The Christian History of The American Revolution: Consider and Ponder, compiled by Verna M. Hall, with an Index of Leading Ideas by Rosalie J. Slater (San Francisco, CA: Foundation for American Christian Education, 1976), pp. 536-543.

Rev. Jones examined parallels between the histories of ancient Israel and the American Colonies. He knew if we were a "virtuous people" we would be a "brave, heroic ... formidable and invincible" people. Then he explained why it was not sinful for the Americans to fight a defensive war.

> To prove, that in some cases, when a people are oppressed, insulted and abused, and can have no other redress, it then becomes our duty as men, with our eyes to GOD, to fight for our liberties and properties; or in other words, that *a defensive war is sinless* before GOD, consequently to engage therein, is consistent with the purest religion.

> If . . . the united voice of all kingdoms, that now or ever have existed, could be admitted as a proof, the point would easily be determined; for there has been no kingdom . . . [that has not] embraced it as their common creed, that a defensive war is innocent. . . .

> Among all the ancient servants of GOD none is more famous for true piety and pure religion than the patriarch Abraham . . . and yet we find this great, this holy man firmly of the faith that a defensive war is sinless. . . . Melchizedeck, the priest of the most high GOD, met him. And did he reprove or curse him? No . . . "he brought forth the bread and wine," giving him the highest expression of approbation, he thus addressed him, viz. "Blessed be Abraham of the Most High GOD, possessor of heaven and earth, and blessed be the Most High GOD, which hath delivered thine enemies into thine hand" (Genesis 14:18-20). . . .

> Moses is of the same faith . . . "he was faithful in all things"; yet we find him often engaged in bloody battles.

... David, a man eminent for pure religion, the sweet psalmist of Israel, David, a man after GOD's own heart, yet all his life is a scene of war. . . .

This indeed is generally acknowledged, when our dispute is with a foreign enemy, but at present it seems like a house divided against itself; our dispute is with administration. This is cause of great sorrow, that such a heavy burden has befallen the kingdom; and yet we are not without some instances in Scripture of people refusing obedience to kings, when they became arbitrary and oppressive. When Rehoboam threatened Israel with nothing but tyranny, they did not long hesitate till they gave the king his answer, "What portion have we in David? Neither have we inheritance in the son of Jesse: To your tents, oh Israel! Now see to thine own house David" (1 Kings 12:16). . . .

And this certainly has been the faith of Great Britain. . . . When King James II departed from the constitution, and became arbitrary . . . the people esteemed it no sin to invite William, the prince of Orange, to invade England, and obliged James to abdicate a kingdom he had forfeited his right to govern. . . .

Pharaoh, king of Egypt . . . enjoined it as a law to all the midwives, that they should kill all the male-children of the Jews. Did they obey or not? The text informs us that the fear of GOD prevented them, believing that no law can make that just, which in its own nature is unrighteous.[84]

---

[84] Ibid.

Rev. Jones explained that a defensive war against a tyrannical government was equal to the "legal process against a criminal."

> (L)aws are not good, except they secure every man's liberty and property, and defend the subject against the arbitrary power of kings, or any body of men whatsoever.
>
> . . . The reason why a defensive war seems so awful to good people, is, they esteem it to be some kind of murder: but this is a very great mistake; for it is no more murder than a legal process against a criminal. The end is the same, the mode is different. In some cases it is the only mode left to obtain justice. And surely that religion is not from heaven, which is against justice on earth. . . . (C)onsider that the design of laws is to punish evil-doers,—to bring to justice offenders, and to secure the innocent in the peaceable possession of their properties: for this end GOD has ordained these higher powers; but it some times has been the case, that those, in whose hands these powers are entrusted, become tyrannical, and the greatest offenders, and shall they live with impunity? GOD forbid! . . . Surely both reason and revelation will justify you in seeking for justice in that mode by which it can be obtained. . . . (H)e that is not clear in conscience to gird on his sword, if he would act consistently, must never sit on a jury to condemn a criminal.[85]

Rev. Jones believed that fighting in self-defense to restore a just government was consistent with true religion, and helped Americans see the choice they must make.

---

[85] Ibid.

We have no choice left to us, but to submit to absolute slavery or despotism, or as free-men to stand in our own defence, and endeavour a noble resistance. Matters are at last brought to this deplorable extremity;—every reasonable method of reconciliation has been tried in vain;—our addresses to our king have been treated with neglect and contempt.... All is at stake—we can appeal to GOD, that we believe our cause is just and good.[86]

Having made it clear that their cause was just, and they must fight with all their might, Rev. Jones assured Americans that if they put their trust in the LORD for victory, and reformed their lives, they would win the war and gain their liberty.

It is probable that most will acknowledge, that the call to arms is alarming, but we are comparatively weak to Great Britain.... (N)o argument is greater than our text, viz. "Remember the LORD is great and terrible" [Nehemiah 1:5]. All human aid is subject to disappointment, but when our dependence is on the almighty God, we may have hope of success, "for the eyes of the LORD run to and fro throughout the whole earth, to shew Himself strong in behalf of them whose heart is perfect towards Him" (2 Chronicles 16:9).... GOD alone is truly great, and greatly to be feared [Psalm 89:7; 96:4].... The Spirit of GOD coming on him (Saul) was a presage of success. And has not the same Spirit come on us? A martial spirit from GOD has spread throughout the land.... There is only one consideration that is very discouraging, and that is the great and many sins that prevail in

---

[86] Ibid.

our land. .... (I)f we are successful in our present struggle for liberty, we cannot expect to enjoy any lasting happiness without a reformation, and a life worthy of the glorious gospel. .... (W)e fight not for present profit, no, our noble struggle is for liberty itself, without which even life would be miserable.[87]

Rev. Samuel West, on 29 May 1776, in his sermon before the Massachusetts-Bay government, said he believed Providence was acting on our behalf, and that He "designed this continent to be the asylum of liberty and true religion."

Many have been the interpositions of Divine Providence on our behalf, both in our fathers' days and ours. .... And can we think that He who has thus far helped us will give us up into the hands of our enemies? Certainly He that began to deliver us will continue to show His mercy towards us, in saving us from the hands of our enemies; He will not forsake us if we do not forsake Him. Our cause is so just and good that nothing can prevent our success but only our sins. .... (Y)et I cannot help hoping, and even believing, that Providence has designed this continent to be the asylum of liberty and true religion; for can we suppose that the God who created us free agents, and designed that we should glorify and serve Him in this world that we might enjoy Him forever hereafter, will suffer liberty and true religion to be banished from off the face of the earth.[88]

---

[87] Ibid.

[88] Op. cit., Samuel West, "A Sermon Preached before the Honorable Council, and the Honorable House of Representatives," pp. 311, 313.

Then Rev. West said the American Colonies needed to move quickly to become "an independent state."

> Having thus endeavored to show the lawfulness and necessity of defending ourselves against the tyranny of Great Britain, I would observe that Providence seems plainly to point to us the expediency, and even necessity, of our considering ourselves an independent state.[89]

Five weeks later, on 2 July 1776, the Continental Congress approved *The Unanimous Declaration of the Thirteen United States of America* (signed July 4), uniting the Americans as one people, independent of Great Britain. There are parallels between the first and last paragraphs of the *Declaration*, and the main points of the sermons above. The *Declaration* contains a long list of violations of the Laws of Nature and of Nature's God committed by the king of England or his representatives. Each violation represented an act of tyranny by which the king failed to function as a magistrate. The last paragraph is an appeal to God for His protection and blessing, because Americans believed their cause was just—which these clergy declared in their sermons.

Rev. John Hurt (1752-1824) was chaplain to General Weedon's brigade during the War for Independence, and preached to the troops in New Jersey. His sermon, *The Love Of Our Country,* must have greatly encouraged the soldiers.

> We have never yet been conquered; we never yet tamely received laws from a tyrant nor never will, while the cause of religion, the cause of nature and of nature's God cry aloud, or even whisper resistance to an oppressor's execrated power.... Let us, then, not build too much upon human prospects, or shut God

---

[89] Ibid.

out of our councils and designs; but let us flee humbly to Him for succor in a pious acknowledgement that without Him nothing is strong, that without Him no king can be saved by the multitude of an host, nor the mightiest man be delivered by his strength.... (L)et us choose on our part the LORD of lords for our God and for our king.[90]

Americans deliberately chose to reject the arbitrary rule of the king of England and Parliament, and to uphold the "LORD of lords" as their only King. Their cry was: "No king but King Jesus!" By this they meant that He alone had absolute sovereignty over them. It did not mean they were planning to set up a civil government with Jesus as their civil king, or that churches were going to control the government.

In 1779, Dr. Samuel Stillman briefly summarized America's attitude toward the War for Independence:

> We are engaged in a most important contest; not for power, but freedom. We mean not to change our masters, but to secure to ourselves, and to generations yet unborn, the perpetual enjoyment of civil and religious liberty, in their fullest extent.[91]

The War for Independence was an act of self-defense, not an act of rebellion. The American people appealed to the Ruler of Nations for a lawful government, and for preservation of their religious and civil liberties. They put their trust in God, and engaged the battle. They were deeply concerned for their posterity because there was no other

---

[90] John Hurt, Chaplain to General Weedon's brigade, "The Love of Our Country. A sermon preached before the troops in New Jersey. Dedicated to Major-General Stephen, and the officers and soldiers of the Virginia battalions" (Printed in 1777). Reprinted in op. cit., Patriot Preachers, pp. 151, 156; full sermon: pp. 143-157.

[91] Op. cit., Samuel Stillman, "The Duty of Magistrates," p. 275.

land in the world that people could flee to as an asylum for liberty. If Americans did not win the battle for liberty and free government, they feared it would be lost for all mankind.

How should we then respond to restore and preserve what they sacrificed to give us?

## BIBLE STUDY:

1. Read the Scriptures quoted or referred to by the clergy in this chapter:
   - Genesis 14:18-20
   - 1 Kings 12:16
   - Nehemiah 1:5; 4:14
   - 2 Chronicles 16:9
   - Psalm 89:7; 96:4
   - Romans 13:1-5
   - Galatians 5:1

2. What did Rev. Jones observe about Abraham, Moses and David?

   ......................................................................................................

## QUESTIONS FOR CONTEMPLATION OR DISCUSSION:

1. Dr. Mayhew's sermon marked the 100th anniversary of what event in England similar to the Revolution in the American Colonies?

   ......................................................................................................

2. What occurred in both nations in response to tyranny?

   ......................................................................................................

3. Who led the noble and just response to tyranny to restore lawful government?

   ......................................................................................................

4. Did the American clergy believe that Americans defending themselves in war against Great Britain was just and sinless, or not? ........................... . Why or why not?

    ................................................................................................................

5. Rev. Jones explained that a defensive war against a tyrannical government was equal to the:

    ................................................................................................................

6. What parallel did Rev. Jones draw between girding "on a sword" to defend one's nation, including against a tyrant, and sitting "on a jury?"

    ................................................................................................................

7. Rev. Jones, in comparing the history of ancient Israel, understood that if Americans were a "virtuous people," they would be:

    ................................................................................................................

8. Rev. Jones said: "We have no choice left to us, but

    ................................................................................................................ "

9. After reminding Americans of God's Providential purpose for their land and His many interpositions on their behalf, what did Rev. West say the Americans must quickly do?

    ................................................................................................................

10. What was the cry of the Americans: "No king but ........................."

11. For what purpose did Rev. Stillman say Americans were fighting for Independence?

    ................................................................................................................

12. Read and discuss the 1776 *Unanimous Declaration of the Thirteen United States of America (Declaration of Independence)*.

## SERMON OUTLINE SUGGESTION:

1. What is the truth about the American Revolution?
2. How was it similar to the English revolution against King Charles?
3. Why did American clergy support the War for Independence?
4. What Scriptural, righteous, just, and faith principles are evident in the 1776 *Declaration of Independence*?

# CHAPTER TWELVE

# The Sin of Slavery
# & The Civil War

S LAVERY IN AMERICA WAS INCONSISTENT WITH THE foundational principles of the United States, and clashed with God's purpose for America. Our Forefathers proclaimed that God had set aside America as an asylum for liberty—not just for people from England, but for people from any nation. And that from this new nation, the light of the Gospel of Jesus Christ and the kingdom of God, and religious and civil liberty, would go forth to every nation of people. This was God's plan for America. But as the Enemy of our souls sought to enslave Adam and Eve and undermine God's plan for them in the Garden of Eden, so also it was his plan to destroy the light of Christ and hope of liberty in America through the bondage of slavery.

The battle for liberty in America began with the first settlements, in the early 1600s. The Pilgrims in Plymouth, Massachusetts, built their settlement on faith in God and the principles of liberty, equality, and self-government. By contrast, fortune seekers who first came to Jamestown, Virginia, prepared the way for slavery, as those who were wealthy sought to make their fellow men into unpaid servants, and welcomed the first slave ship that landed in 1619.

It should not be surprising that most of the sermons during the mid- and late-1700s which kindled the FIRE for liberty and self-government came from New England, where the vast majority opposed slavery. Opposition to slavery also existed in other American Colonies. There were pastors in Maryland and southern Colonies who spoke against slavery, and exhorted masters to respect the religious rights of their slaves and to treat them with dignity.

Rev. Thomas Bacon, minister of the Protestant Episcopal Church in Maryland, delivered several sermons under the title, *Sermons Addressed To Masters And Servants*, published in 1743. He did not have the power to abolish slavery, but he could speak against it and defend the humanity and God-given rights of the slaves. Thus he spoke about the spiritual duties of masters toward their servants, and exhorted the former to remember that both have the same Maker and LORD. Although it was impossible to prevent people from praying or meeting in secret, masters did determine whether their slaves could go to church or receive an education. These were violations of their God-given rights. Rev. Bacon said,

> Colossians 4:1 "Masters give unto your Servants that which is just and equal, knowing that ye also have a Master in Heaven." . . .

> (E)very service or help which one man affords another, requires its corresponding return [in pay or compensation]. . . .

> (A) principal branch of this duty [is] *The indispensable obligation* every Master and Mistress lies under, of bringing up their slaves in the knowledge and fear of Almighty God. . . .

> Our blessed Saviour Himself, who died for all, and *would have all men* to be saved, and to come unto the knowledge of the truth (*1 Timothy 2:4*), hath a near personal interest in it: as the souls I now would recommend to your care have an equal share with ours in His most precious blood, and [are] consequently dear to Him.[92]

---

[92] Op. cit., Thomas Bacon, "Sermons Addressed to Masters and Servants," pp. 1-5.

Rev. Bacon encouraged masters to fulfill their obligation to educate "their slaves in the knowledge and fear of Almighty God," by giving them Sundays off to attend church and rest from their labors.

> The seventh day was set apart as a day of rest and devotion; not only as a memorial of the creation, but to the *Israelites* was also to be a perpetual remembrance of their delivery from the bondage of the *Egyptians*:—Whence the precept of resting on the Sabbath is said to relate to servants in particular; *viz. that thy man-servant and thy maid-servant may rest as well as thou (Deuteronomy 5:14). ... The* LORD's *Day* ... our servants have an equal title to the benefits of it. . . . How much more then ought we to labour, that our slaves may partake of the blessings of the Gospel; and thereby be enabled to *enter into* that *everlasting* rest of the people of God *(Hebrews 4:11), which they have as much right* to as we have?[93]

Bishop Richard Allen (1760-1831) was one of the earliest black leaders in American history. He was born a slave, devoted his life to Christ at an early age, and was later set free. He was an eminently godly man, without malice toward others, despite the things he suffered. He became a minister of the Gospel, rose to leadership, and was a founder of the African Methodist Episcopal Church. Here are some excerpts from his biography.

---

[93] Ibid.

"Mark the perfect man, and behold the upright: for the end of that man is peace" (Psalm 37:37)....

I was born in the year of our LORD 1760, on February 14th, a slave to Benjamin Chew, of Philadelphia. My mother and father and four children of us were sold into Delaware state, near Dover; and I was a child and lived with him until I was upwards of twenty years of age, during which time I was awakened and brought to see myself, poor, wretched and undone, and without the mercy of God must be lost. Shortly after, I obtained mercy through the blood of Christ, and was constrained to exhort my old companions to seek the LORD....

My master was an unconverted man, all the family, but he was what the world called a good master. He was more like a father to his slaves than anything else.... My oldest brother embraced religion and my sister. Our neighbors, seeing that our [new] master indulged us with the privilege of attending meeting once in two weeks, said that Stokeley's Negroes would soon ruin him; and so my brother and myself held a council together, that we would attend more faithfully to our master's business, so that it should not be said that religion made us worse servants; we would work night and day to get our crops forward, so that they should be disappointed. . . . At length, our master said he was convinced that religion made slaves better and not worse, and often boasted of his slaves for their honesty and industry. Some time after, I asked him if I might ask the preachers to come and preach at his house. . . . Preaching continued for some months; at length, Freeborn Garrettson preached from these words, "Thou art weighed in the balance, and art found wanting." In pointing out and weighing the different characters, and among the rest weighed the slaveholders, my master believed himself to be one of that number, and after that he could not be satisfied to hold slaves, believing it to be wrong. . . .

We left our master's house . . . While living with him we had family prayer in the kitchen . . . At length he invited us from the kitchen to the parlor to hold family prayer . . . We had our stated times to hold our prayer meetings and give exhortations in the neighborhood.[94]

---

[94] Richard Allen, <u>The Life Experience and Gospel Labors of the Rt. Rev. Richard Allen, to which is annexed the Rise and Progress of the African Methodist Episcopal Church in the United States of America. Containing a Narrative of the Yellow Fever in the Year of Our Lord 1793. With an Address to the People of Color in the United States</u>. Written by himself, and Published by his request. With an Introduction by George A. Singleton (NY/Nashville: Abingdon Press, 1960), pp. 15-18. [Howard University, School of Divinity: BX 8449 A6 A3 1960]

Richard Allen soon became a preacher, and later a leader of the black Christians in Philadelphia. Due to persecution from white church elders and leaders who attempted to restrict the religious liberty and independent worship of the black people, Rev. Allen and others formed a new congregation named Bethel Church. He was its first pastor, and was a fine Christian man who held no bitterness toward those who misused their authority and misrepresented Christ.

Years later, in 1816, Rev. Allen and other black leaders who recognized that blacks in other cities suffered the same persecutions, called for a convention of delegates from their respective churches. At the convention, they resolved, "That the people of Philadelphia, Baltimore, etc., should become one body, under the name of the African Methodist Episcopal (A.M.E.) Church." Thus, a new denomination was formed.[95]

Dr. Samuel Stillman spoke about the evil of slavery to the public officials of Massachusetts Bay, in his sermon titled, *The Duty of Magistrates*. When he preached in 1779, America was already in the fifth year of the War for Independence. Dr. Stillman believed slavery was a violation of the foundational principles of the nation, and strikingly inconsistent with their fight for freedom. New England remained a safe haven for former slaves because most citizens there believed the practice was morally wrong. Since Americans united together as one people, the New England clergy began to call for the elimination of slavery in all the Colonies.

> In order to ... be consistent with ourselves, it appears to me that we ought to banish from among us that cruel practice, which has long prevailed, of reducing to a state of slavery for life the freeborn Africans.
>
> The Deity hath bestowed upon them and us the same natural rights as men; and hath assigned to them a

[95] Ibid., pp. 26-35.

part of the globe for their residence. But mankind, urged by those passions which debase the human mind, have pursued them to their native country; and by fomenting wars among them, that they might secure the prisoners, or employing villains to decoy the unwary, have filled their ships with the unfortunate captives; dragged them from their tenderest connections, and transported them to different parts of the earth, to be hewers of wood, and drawers of water, till death shall end their painful captivity.

To reconcile this nefarious traffic with reason, humanity, religion, or the principles of a free government, in my view, requires uncommon address.

Should we make the case our own, and act agreeably to that excellent rule of our blessed LORD, *Whatever ye would that men should do to you, do ye to them likewise* [Luke 6:31], the abolition of this disgraceful practice would take place.

Shall we hold the sword in one hand to defend our just rights as men; and grasp chains with the other to enslave the inhabitants of Africa? Forbid it heaven!— Forbid it all the freeborn sons of this western world![96]

Rev. David Rice (1733-1816) spent many years preaching and traveling in Virginia, North Carolina, and Kentucky, during which he observed the cruelty of slavery. As an elected member of the Kentucky Constitutional Convention in 1792, he delivered a speech titled, *Slavery Inconsistent With Justice and Good Policy.* During the convention, he believed it was his duty before God to oppose slavery

---

[96] Op. cit., Samuel Stillman, "The Duty of Magistrates," pp. 284-286.

and thoroughly state the reasons why it should be prohibited by the state constitution.

> Sir, I have lived free, and in many respects happy for near sixty years; but my happiness has been greatly diminished, for much of the time, by hearing a great part of the human species groaning under the galling yoke of bondage. In this time I lost a venerable father, a tender mother, two affectionate sisters, and a beloved first born son; but all these together have not cost me half the anxiety as has been occasioned by this wretched situation of my fellow-men, whom without a blush I call my brethren. When I consider their deplorable state, and who are the cause of their misery, the load of misery that lies on them, and the load of guilt on us for imposing it on them; it fills my soul with anguish. I view their distresses, I read the anger of Heaven, I believe that if I should not exert myself, when, and as far, as in my power, in order to relieve them, I should be partaker of the guilt....

> Sir, the question is, Whether slavery is consistent with justice and good policy?...

> (T)here are some cases, where a man may justly be made a slave by law. By a vicious conduct he may forfeit his freedom; he may forfeit his life. Where this is the case, and the safety of the public may be secured by reducing the offender to a state of slavery, it will be right; it may be an act of kindness. In no other case, if my conceptions are just, can it be vindicated on principles of justice or humanity....

> As creatures of God we are, with respect to liberty, all equal. If one has a right to live among his fellow

creatures, and enjoy his freedom, so has another; if one has a right to enjoy property he acquires by an honest industry, so has another. If I by force take that from another, which he has a just right to according to the law of nature (which is a divine law) which he has never forfeited, and to which he has never relinquished his claim, I am certainly guilty of injustice and robbery; and when the thing taken is the man's liberty, when it is himself, it is the greatest injustice.

. . . (A) slave, being a free moral agent, and an accountable creature (to his Maker), is a capable subject of religion and morality; . . . (However, it) is in the power of the master to deprive him of all the means of religious and moral instruction, either in private or in public. Some masters have actually exercised this power, and restrained their slaves from the means of instruction, by the terror of the lash. Slaves have not opportunity, at their own disposal . . . it is put out of their power to learn to read . . . Masters designedly keep their slaves in ignorance lest they should become too knowing to answer their selfish purposes; and too wise to rest easy in their degraded situation. In this case the law operates so as to answer an end directly opposed to the proper end of all law. . . . It supports in a land of religious liberty, the severest persecutions and may operate so as totally to rob multitudes of their religious privileges and the rights of conscience. . . .

In America, a slave is a standing monument of the tyranny and inconsistency of human governments. . . .

He is declared by the united voice of America [in the *Declaration of Independence*, the editor presumes], to be by nature free, and entitled to the privilege of acquiring and enjoying property; and yet by the laws passed and enforced in these states, retained in slavery, and dispossessed of all property and capacity of acquiring any. They have furnished a striking instance of a people carrying on a war in defence of principles, which they are actually and avowedly destroying by legal force; using one measure for themselves and another for their neighbors. . . .

Consistent justice is the solid basis on which the fabric of government will rest securely; take this away, and the building totters, and is liable to fall before every blast. It is, I presume, the avowed principles of each of us, that all men are by nature free, and are still entitled to freedom, unless they forfeited it. . . .

Slavery naturally tends to sap the foundations of moral, and consequently of political virtue; and virtue is absolutely necessary for the happiness and prosperity of a free people. . . .

The owners of such slaves then are the licensed robbers, and not the just proprietors, of what they claim; freeing them is not depriving them of property, but restoring it to the right owner; it is suffering the unlawful captive to escape. It is not wronging the master, but doing justice to the slave, restoring him to himself. The master, it is true, is wronged, he may suffer and that greatly; but this is his own fault, and the fault of the enslaving law; and not of the law that does justice to the oppressed. . . .

Human legislatures should remember, that they act in subordination to the great Ruler of the universe, have no right to take the government out of His hand nor to enact laws contrary to His; that if they should presume to attempt it, they cannot make that right, which He has made wrong; they cannot dissolve the allegiance of His subjects, and transfer it to themselves, and thereby free the people from their obligations to obey the laws of nature. The people should know, that legislatures have not this power; and a thousand laws can never make that innocent, which the divine law has made criminal; or give them a right to that, which the divine law forbids them to claim.

. . . (T)herefore I give it as my opinion, that the first thing to be done is TO RESOLVE, UNCONDITIONALLY, TO PUT AN END TO SLAVERY IN THIS STATE. This, I conceive, properly belongs to the convention; which they can easily effect, by working the principle into the constitution they are to frame. . . .

The slavery of the Negroes began in iniquity; a curse has attended it, and a curse will follow it. National vices will be punished with national calamities. Let us avoid these vices, that we may avoid the punishment which they deserve; and endeavor so to act, as to secure the approbation and smiles of heaven.[97]

The Kentucky Constitutional Convention as a whole heeded only part of Rev. Rice's plea by placing some restrictions on slavery.

---

[97] David Rice, "Slavery Inconsistent with Justice and Good Policy," delivered before the Kentucky Constitutional Convention in Augusta, Kentucky, 1792. Reprinted in op. cit., American Political Writing, 2:859-860, 863, 866-867, 870-871, 879-880, 882; full sermon: 2:858-883.

However, they did not have the conviction or courage to adopt his full proposal, though I expect they knew he was right. The decision of the Convention cost the lives of many thousands of their posterity during the Civil War.

## Slavery, War for Independence, & Constitutional Convention

God allowed the horrendous institution of slavery to continue in America for many generations. During the War for Independence, the Americans appealed to God for assistance and He helped them gain their freedom. He did so even though they had not set their slaves free. Many Americans opposed slavery and realized it was inconsistent with their convictions and ideals, as stated in the *Declaration of Independence* and some State constitutions. Others, especially from southern States, supported slavery because of their contrary beliefs and economic dependence upon slaves.

During the War for Independence, representatives from the States set up their first form of national government under the *Articles of Confederation*. Within a few years, they realized it could not work effectively. It had no executive or judicial branches, and no means of enforcing legislative directives. Consequently, the thirteen Colonies sent representatives to a Constitutional Convention in 1787, at which they developed a plan for a new form of federal government. As they neared completion of the draft *Constitution of the United States of America*, the Convention hit a roadblock when they could not come to agreement about slavery. Slavery became so divisive that many representatives feared the issue would prevent acceptance of the new form of government. If they didn't approve the *Constitution* for ratification, the States could not long be preserved as a union. Representatives from southern States declared they would not support the *Constitution* if it forbade slavery. Consequently, the delegates worked out a compromise that the "migration or importation" of slaves could not be prohibited for 20 years.[98] By 1788, nine States ratified the *Constitution*, and the new government was soon formed.

The national Constitutional Convention successfully avoided full confrontation on slavery, but at great cost to future generations. They could have stopped slavery in 1776 or in 1787. They had seen the hand of Providence intervene on their behalf in numerous impossible situations before, during, and after the War for Independence. The LORD had given them wisdom, courage, and assistance in their conflict with Great Britain. He also helped them during the Constitutional Convention, when they sought Him directly for the wisdom necessary to create a new government, inspiring them to create the best form of government known to mankind. Why did they not implore Him for wisdom as to how to end slavery, especially for how the South could survive economically without slave labor?

## Providential Intervention

Let me share with you a providential event that came to my understanding in the Library of Congress while I was researching these matters. Recognizing that the 20-year moratorium would end in 1808, I searched through the Congressional Records from 1789 until 1808. I discovered four slave trade acts, passed during the terms of the first four presidents: George Washington, John Adams, Thomas Jefferson, James Madison. These federal laws placed various restrictions on slavery outside the Southern slave States (e.g., prohibiting American ships to transport slaves). The biggest was the 1806-1807 slave trade bill. Then I looked at the 1808 records. Since Congress was only in session for 3-4 months during those years, they adjourned near the end of April, without passing any legislation to end slavery nationwide. I was shocked! It was clear to me that Congress lacked the courage to do anything to restrict or end slavery in States where it existed.

---

[98] United States Constitution, Art. I, Sec. 9, Par. 1; see also, Art. V.

Then thoughts entered my mind that appeared entirely unrelated to the research. The Spirit of the LORD whispered in my mind, "to the very day." I immediately knew this referred to the time when the LORD delivered Israel out of bondage of slavery in Egypt after 430 years "to the very day" (Exodus 12:41). Moses led the Israelites out of slavery, but he was born 80 years earlier. He was prepared for this role through 40 years in Pharaoh's household, and then 40 years in the wilderness as a shepherd. Then I realized the Creator God was working out His plan long before: when He ordained the timing of Moses' birth, and the daughter of Pharaoh to rescue him from death.

So, I stood pondering how any of those historical truths were related to the abolition of slavery in the United States? I could not remember anything significantly related to this issue in 1808, so I began thinking about historical events in 1809. Then I remembered the date of 12 February 1809, and realized it was just over nine months after Congress went out of session in 1808. Immediately the revelation came: corresponding with her menstrual cycle, the mother of Abraham Lincoln conceived him within her womb after Congress adjourned and had not ended slavery in the United States. It was he who became our 16th President, and led the nation through the Civil War. Halfway through his first term, on 1 January 1863, he issued the *Emancipation Proclamation*, declaring that "all persons held as slaves within any State . . . are forever free."[99]

## President Lincoln on the Cause of the Civil War

President Lincoln's *Second Inaugural Address*, delivered on 4 March 1865 (42 days before he was assassinated), is inscribed on the north wall of the Lincoln Memorial. The address was short, but focused on the cause of the Civil War.

---

[99] Abraham Lincoln, U.S. President, "Proclamation. By the President of the United States of America," January 1, 1863. Op. cit., <u>A Compilation of the Messages and Papers of the Presidents</u>, 5:3358-3360.

One-eighth of the whole population were colored slaves, not distributed generally over the Union, but localized in the southern part of it. These slaves constituted a peculiar and powerful interest. All knew that this interest was somehow the cause of the war. To strengthen, perpetuate, and extend this interest was the object for which the insurgents would rend the Union even by war, while the Government claimed no right to do more than to restrict the territorial enlargement of it. . . . Both read the same Bible and pray to the same God, and each invokes His aid against the other. It may seem strange that any men should dare to ask a just God's assistance in wringing their bread from the sweat of other men's faces, but let us judge not, that we be not judged. The prayers of both could not be answered. That of neither has been answered fully. The Almighty has His own purposes. "Woe unto the world because of offenses; for it must needs be that offenses come, but woe to that man by whom the offense cometh" [Matthew 18:7]. If we shall suppose that American slavery is one of those offenses which, in the providence of God, must needs come, but which, having continued through His appointed time, He now wills to remove, and that He gives to both North and South this terrible war as the woe due to those by whom the offense came, shall we discern therein any departure from those divine attributes which the believers in a living God always ascribe to Him? Fondly do we hope, fervently do we pray, that this mighty scourge of war may speedily pass away. Yet, if God wills that it continue until all the wealth piled by the bondsman's two hundred and fifty years of unrequited toil shall be sunk, and until every drop of blood drawn with the lash shall be paid by another drawn with the sword, as was said three thousand years ago, so still it must be said, "the judgments of the LORD are true and righteous altogether."[100] [Psalm 19:9]

Abraham Lincoln believed the Civil War was God's judgment upon the entire nation for slavery. Slavery, not States' rights, was the cause of the Civil War. The southern States made the claim of States' rights in order to claim a right to have and perpetuate slavery. They were willing to destroy the Union to preserve this evil practice, even though before the Civil War, the Federal Government had not prohibited slavery within the slave States. Federal laws had only prohibited slavery outside slave States, plus Congress sought to prohibit it in new territories being added to the Union.

## Impartial Divine Judgment

There were more lives lost in the Civil War than all other United States wars combined. Not including wounded, total Civil War casualties were 624,511. The North (Federal) lost 364,511 men, and the South (Confederate) lost 260,000.[101] If these figures are assessed from a Biblical perspective, it is clear that God viewed both sides responsible for slavery, the cause of the conflict. God did hold the South responsible for the sin of slavery. But equally or more so, He held the North accountable for the 1787 compromise and the unwillingness of Congress to end slavery when it had the authority to

---

[100] Ibid., "Second Inaugural Address," March 4, 1865, A Compilation of the Messages and Papers of the Presidents, 5:3477-3478.

[101] "War Statistics," The Civil War Battlefield Guide, edited by Frances H. Kennedy, produced by The Conservative Fund (Boston: Houghton Mifflin Company, 1990), p. 301.

do so in 1808. Further, the sin of racism still plagues our nation today because there has not yet been nationwide repentance for the sins of slavery and racism.

Today the USA is guilty of a greater sin, a greater evil and injustice: the murder and innocent bloodshed of more than 65 million babies.

## BIBLE STUDY:

1. Review Scriptures quoted by clergy, President Lincoln, or the author:
   - Exodus 12:41;
   - Deuteronomy 5:14;
   - Psalm 19:9;
   - Psalm 37:37;
   - Matthew 18:7;
   - Luke 6:31;
   - Colossians 4:1;
   - 1 Timothy 2:4;
   - Hebrews 4:11.

2. Do a study of slavery in the Bible.
   ...........................................................................................................

3. Do you think slavery, or certain types of slavery, is a sin?
   ...........................................................................................................

4. Did God ever authorize any people to travel to a foreign nation or region and capture people from there and make them, their spouses, and their children lifetime slaves?
   ...........................................................................................................

5. What does the Bible reveal as the most important factor for victory, and for no loss, or low loss, of life in war (Deuteronomy 1:41-45)?
   ...........................................................................................................

6. When Israel lost 36 soldiers – instead of total victory with no loss of life – in a battle against Ai, what did Joshua not know? Why did he tear his clothes and humble himself before God? And why did God correct him (Joshua 7:1-15)?

.............

7. Do you think sin is a cause of war, or elevated numbers of deaths in war?

.............

8. Do you think God uses war to judge nations for their sin?

.............

## QUESTIONS FOR CONTEMPLATION OR DISCUSSION:

1. What practice in the USA was entirely inconsistent with our founding principles?

.............

2. Dr. Stillman asked: "Shall we hold the sword in one hand to defend our just rights as men; and .............
............."

3. What were some reasons that David Rice opposed slavery?

.............

4. What great outcomes came about because of Richard Allen's conversion to Christ, while a slave and during the remainder of his life?

.............

5. What was the compromise in 1787 that led to approval, including by Southern States, of the new *Constitution of the United States of America*?

.............

6. What did God do when the U.S. Congress failed to prohibit slavery after the 20-year moratorium ended?

.............................................................................................................

7. What did President Abraham Lincoln say was the cause of the Civil War?

.............................................................................................................

8. What do the number of war deaths from the North and South reveal about God's impartial judgment?

.............................................................................................................

## SERMON OUTLINE SUGGESTION:

1. Was American slavery a sin?
2. What did God do to end slavery in the United States?
3. Was the Civil War a judgment of God for the sin of slavery?
4. How did clergy and President Lincoln help their fellow Americans understand slavery and the Civil War from a Biblically illuminated understanding?
5. Why is it important for us today to have national repentance for slavery and racism?

# CHAPTER THIRTEEN

# The Cause of Corruption & Method of Restoration of a Nation

REV. DAVID JONES PREACHED A SERMON TITLED, *DEFENSIVE War In A Just Cause Sinless,* on the Day of the Continental Fast, in Chester County, Pennsylvania. The day was 20 July 1775, three months after the War for Independence started. Although he spoke about the war, he was concerned about the spiritual state of the people, for he knew that their sin could subvert America's hopes for liberty and happiness.

> When a people become voluntary slaves to sin; when it is esteemed a reproach to reverence and serve God; when profaneness and dissolute morals become fashionable; when pride and luxury predominate, we cannot expect such a nation to be long happy.[102]

The cause of corruption for individuals and nations is sin. Of the word "sin", *Webster's 1828 Dictionary* observes, "The primary sense is . . . to depart, to wander," and defined it as,

> The voluntary departure of a moral agent from a known rule of rectitude or duty, prescribed by God; . . . Sin is either a [direct] act in which a known

---

[102] Op. cit., David Jones, "Defensive War in a Just Cause Sinless."

divine law is violated, or it is the voluntary neglect
to obey a positive [direct] divine command, or a
rule of duty clearly implied in such command. Sin
comprehends not actions only, but neglect of known
duty, all evil thoughts, purposes, words and desires,
whatever is contrary to God's commands or law. I
John iii. Matt. xv. James iv.[103]

A contemporary example might help us understand sin as a
"voluntary departure" that has bad effects. Automobile manufacturers
use robots in the assembly process. The robots work with perfect
precision, installing parts exactly the same on each car. What if the
robot departed from its programmed instructions, and installed parts
in wrong places? Can you imagine the robot choosing not to install
a part, or switching the front and rear fenders? Any departure from
the programmer's instructions would be a malfunction, and the robot
would be stopped immediately. The programmer would repair the
malfunction and place the robot back in service.

God did not make us like programmed robots, but He did write
His laws and instructions on our hearts, and gave them to us in written
form in the Bible. We know what we are supposed to do, but have a
sinful nature pushing us in the opposite direction, yet God will not
force us to do what is right. We are free to obey or not obey Him.
When our hearts are right before Him, and we follow His commands
out of love for Him, we live in harmony with Him, have peace in
our souls, feel good about ourselves, and enjoy the blessings of right
relationships with other people. When we ignore His promptings
or disobey His commands, we are not in harmony with Him, lose
peace, feel bad about ourselves, and have broken relationships. Sin is
always at the door, and always destructive of our relationships with
God and people (Genesis 4:6-7). If we do not stop that destruction by
repentance, forgiveness, reconciliation, and obedience, it eats away at

---

[103] Op. cit., Noah Webster, An American Dictionary, s.v. "sin."

us like a cancer. "For the wages of sin is death, but the free gift of God is eternal life in Christ Jesus our LORD" (Romans 6:23).

God does not stop us from sinning like a programmer can stop a robot when it malfunctions. If we are listening to His voice, He speaks gently to us, encouraging us in the right path. If we are tempted to go astray, He pricks our conscience, and sends warning signals. If we fail to listen to and obey His gentle voice, then He may put obstacles in our path to direct us back to Him, where He offers forgiveness and renewal through Christ Jesus. His desire is that we increasingly think and act the way He does, and the way He designed us to, which enables us to have joy and right relationships with Him and people. He did create us in His image and likeness (Genesis 1:26-27)! His purpose in correcting or judging us is to restore us to Himself and others, not to condemn us. He is our Father God! Nevertheless, until we die and stand before Him on the Day of Judgment, the decision is ours as to how we will respond, and whether we will align ourselves with His will. He is always inviting us into intimate relationship with Him, but it is up to us whether we listen and respond to His voice.

We are not a happy nation today. Instead, we are self-destructing. Perhaps Rev. Jones saw the early signs of degeneration, which have come to full fruition in recent generations, especially in recent years. As a clergyman, he fulfilled his duty to warn the people of their sinful ways and the consequences. He knew that it was not a crime, but it was a sin, to become "slaves of sin," discourage reverence toward God, be prideful, or be obsessed with gaining material possessions. Yet he also knew that a nation enslaved to these desires and sins could not "be long happy" or free. We have become the nation he hoped we would not.

In Dr. Samuel Langdon's 1775 sermon titled, *Government Corrupted By Vice, and Recovered By Righteousness*, he explained man's tendency to forget God, toward vice and corruption, and that corrupt people will get corrupt leaders. He also knew what was necessary to restore an individual or a nation to God.

> Let us consider—that for the sins of a people God
> may suffer the best government to be corrupted or
> entirely dissolved, and that nothing but a general
> reformation can give good ground to hope that the
> public happiness will be restored by the recovery
> of the strength and perfection of the state, and that
> Divine Providence interpose to fill every department
> with wise and good men.[104]

In generations past, we had "the best government" known to
mankind. Even so, God allowed it "to be corrupted" because of sin.
Dr. Langdon continued by providing insights from the history of
Judah that are applicable today.

> The whole body of the nation, from head to foot,
> was full of moral and political disorders, without
> any remaining soundness. Their religion was all
> mere ceremony and hypocrisy; and even the laws of
> common justice and humanity were disregarded in
> their public courts. They had counselors and judges,
> but very different from those at the beginning of
> the commonwealth. Their princes were rebellious
> against God and the constitution of their country,
> and companions of thieves—giving countenance
> to every artifice for seizing the property of the
> subjects into their own hands, and robbing the
> public treasury. Every one loved gifts, and followed
> after rewards; they regarded the perquisites [fees
> paid them or benefits beyond ordinary salary] more
> than the duties of office; the general aim was at
> profitable places and pensions; they were influenced
> in everything by bribery and their avarice and luxury

---

[104] Op. cit., Samuel Langdon, "Government Corrupted by Vice, and Recovered
by Righteousness," pp. 238-242, 255.

were never satisfied, but hurried them on to all kinds of oppression and violence, so that they even justified and encouraged the murder of innocent persons to support their lawless power and increase their wealth. And God, in righteous judgment, left them to run into all this excess of vice, to their own destruction, because they had forsaken Him, and were guilty of willful inattention to the most essential parts of that religion which had been given them by a well-attested revelation from heaven.[105]

Although written about 250 years ago, Dr. Langdon's words read like an indictment of our nation and political leaders today. He continued by describing American history before it happened.

(V)ice will increase with the riches and glory of an empire; and this gradually tends to corrupt the constitution, and in time bring on its dissolution. This may be considered not only as the natural effect of vice, but a righteous judgment of Heaven, especially upon a nation which has been favored with the blessings of religion and liberty, and is guilty of undervaluing them, and eagerly going into the gratification of every lust.[106]

The United States has "been favored with" countless blessings, but we are unquestionably "guilty of undervaluing them" and gratifying every lustful desire. Dr. Langdon spoke of the reformation we need in our land.

Yet if a general reformation of religion and morals had taken place [in Judah during the time of Jeremiah],

---

[105] Ibid.
[106] Ibid.

and they had turned to God from their sins,—if they had again recovered the true spirit of their religion,—God, by the gracious interpositions of His providence, would soon have found out methods to restore the former virtue of the state, and again have given them men of wisdom and integrity, according to their utmost wish, to be counselors and judges. This was verified in fact after the nation had been purged by a long captivity, and returned to their own land humbled and filled with zeal for God and His law.[107]

Dr. Langdon concluded with an exhortation and prayer for the members of the Massachusetts-Bay Congress.

On your wisdom, religion, and public spirit, honored gentlemen, we depend. . . . May God be with you, and by the influences of His Spirit direct all your counsels and resolutions for the glory of His name and the safety and happiness of this colony. We have great reason to acknowledge with thankfulness the evident tokens of the Divine presence. . . . It is our earnest prayer to the Father of Lights that He would eradicate your minds, make all your way plain, and grant you may be happy instruments of many and great blessings to the people by whom you are constituted, to New England, and all the united colonies.[108]

In 1769, Rev. Amos Adams preached two discourses on *The perils, Hardships, Difficulties and Discouragements which have Attended the Planting and Progressive Improvements of New-England.* He delivered

---

[107] Ibid.
[108] Ibid.

them on a day for a General Fast, quoting passages of Scripture as texts for his sermon. Each contains a warning, encouragement, or instruction.

> "So now, take your stand, that I may plead with you before the LORD concerning all the righteous acts of the LORD which He did for you and your fathers" (1 Samuel 12:7).

> "To grant us that we, being delivered from the hand of our enemies, might serve Him without fear, in holiness and righteousness before Him all our days" (Luke 1:74-75).

> "For He established a testimony in Jacob, and appointed a law in Israel, which He commanded our fathers, that they should teach them to their children . . . that they should put their confidence in God, and not forget the works of God, but keep His commandments" (Psalm 78:5, 7).[109]

The first and third passages inform us of the importance of remembering "all the righteous acts of the LORD which He did for" us. Like Israel, we need to know our history, and how God has intervened on our behalf or rendered His righteous judgments. Because most Americans don't know these truths, our nation is making the same errors as ancient Israel, rather than learning from them. How could these clergymen so accurately describe our nation today—especially when America was, in comparison, only mildly corrupt then? They could do so because they knew how easily we, as fallen people, stray from God and are vulnerable to vices.

---

[109] Op. cit., Amos Adams, "A concise, historical view of the perils, hardships, difficulties and discouragements . . . With reflections, *principally*, moral and religious," pp. 1-2, 7-8, 65.

The second passage conveyed Rev. Adams' hope that America would serve God and be a righteous nation.

In the third passage, Rev. Adams exhorted parents to teach their children about God and the works He has done. Parents and teachers were faithful to do this at least until the early 1900s, and the history books were filled with records of events revealing the hand of God in our history. However, beginning around the 1930s, textbook authors, teachers, and others ignored and deliberately removed almost all references to God from most textbooks and curricula. Is it any surprise that the generations who do not know our history do not have confidence in God in relationship to public matters, or see the relevance of His sovereignty or the Scriptures?

Rev. Adams concluded with a warning to our nation that ought to be sounded with a loud trumpet today.

> Let us consider our dependence on God for future prosperity. We have had an awful example of God's severity in rooting out whole nations to make room for us. He caused them to melt away as the dew before the rising sun: Their name and memorial is, in a manner, perished out of the earth. Hath not God the same power over us? If we forsake Him and serve other gods, or serve diverse lusts and pleasures, Divine Providence will cast us out of its protection, we shall sink under the weight of our own sins, as multitudes of ancient kingdoms and nations have done; we shall perish from off the earth. . . . God has judgments enough in store— Fear as well as love ought to engage us to serve God. Corruption and immorality are the natural, necessary ruin of people, and history presents us with striking examples of nations that have sunk under the weight of their own vices.—A people can never be free and happy but in proportion as they

are virtuous—vice is slavery, misery and certain ruin.[110]

Rev. Jedidiah Morse, D.D. (1761-1826), pastor of the Church in Charlestown, delivered a sermon on 25 April 1799, the Day of a National Fast. He titled it, *A Sermon, Exhibiting the Present Dangers, and Consequent Duties of the Citizens of the United States of America.* He sounded an alarm that we ought to sound again today, since the common foundations of our religion and government are being assailed in every way imaginable. He credits "the kindly influence of Christianity" as the source of the freedom and happiness America enjoyed, and draws a direct parallel between its influence and the level of freedom and good government a nation enjoys.

"If the foundations be destroyed, what can the righteous do" (Psalm 11:3)? — If RELIGION and GOVERNMENT, the foundations here meant, be subverted and overthrown, what could the best of men, however righteous their cause, hope to do to any good effect in such a state of things. . . .

---

[110] Ibid.

Believing, as I firmly do, that the foundations of all our *most precious interests* are formidably assailed, and that the subtle and secret assailants are increasing in number, and are multiplying, varying, and arranging their means of attack, it would be criminal in me to be silent. I am compelled to sound the alarm, and I will do it, so far as GOD shall enable me, with fidelity....

Our dangers are two kinds, those which affect our religion, and those which affect our government. They are, however, so closely allied that they cannot, with propriety, be separated. The foundations which support the interests of Christianity, are also necessary to support a free and equal government like our own. In all those countries where there is little or no religion, or a very gross and corrupt one ... there you will find, with scarcely a single exception, arbitrary and tyrannical governments, gross ignorance and wickedness, and deplorable wretchedness among the people. To the kindly influence of Christianity we owe that degree of civil freedom and political and social happiness which mankind now enjoy. In proportion as the genuine effects of Christianity are diminished in any nation, either through unbelief, or the corruption of its doctrines, or the neglect of its institutions; in the same proportion will the people of that nation recede from the blessings of genuine freedom, and approximate the miseries of complete despotism.[111]

---

[111] Jedidiah Morse, D.D., pastor of the Church in Charlestown, "A Sermon, Exhibiting the Present Dangers, and Consequent Duties of the Citizens of the United States of America." Delivered at Charlestown, April 25, 1799. The Day of the National Fast (Charlestown: printed and sold by Samuel Etheridge, 1799), pp. 7, 9; full sermon: 50 pages. [LOC: E 323 .M87 Rare Book Collection]

## BIBLE STUDY:

1. Read the Scriptures quoted by the clergy and the author in this chapter:
   - Genesis 1:26-27;
   - 1 Samuel 12:7;
   - Psalm 11:3;
   - Psalm 78:5, 7;
   - Luke 1:74-75;
   - Romans 6:23.

2. What do the Scriptures referenced in the *Webster's 1828 Dictionary* reveal about sin (1 John 3:4-10; Matthew 15:1-20; James 4:1-17)?

   ...........................................................................................................

3. What were some of the sins committed by Israel and Judah that resulted in their demise and being conquered by their enemies (2 Kings 17:7-23; 21:1-16)?

   ...........................................................................................................

4. What was the national sin that God said He never imagined His own people would do, and He would not forgive, though He did forgive Manasseh personally when he repented (2 Kings 21:6, 16; 24:4; 2 Chronicles 33:1-13; Jeremiah 7:31-34; 19:1-9; 32:35)?

   ...........................................................................................................

5. Does God use enemies, attacks, war and expulsion from their land to judge nations for their sins (2 Kings 17:1-6; 24:1-3)?

   ...........................................................................................................

6. Was repentance for national sins essential before God moved to restore a people or nation (Daniel 9:1-23; Nehemiah 1:4-11)?

   ...........................................................................................................

7. Did God restore the Jews to their homeland after judgment and enable them to rebuild (Daniel 9:1-2; Nehemiah)?

8. Why is it important to know the history of God, of Divine Providence, working in, blessing, correcting, or judging, both in the history of Israel and Judah recorded in the Bible, and in your own nation (Deuteronomy 4:1-40; 6:1-25; Psalm 78; 145)?

9. In Psalm 11:3, David asks, "If the foundations are destroyed, what can the righteous do?" What do the other verses in that Psalm reveal about where the LORD is and what He is doing? And could what He is doing move the nation toward restoration?

10. If there is genuine repentance, personal and national, is there hope for forgiveness, healing and restoration in your nation (Psalm 32; 1 John 1:8-10)?

## QUESTIONS FOR CONTEMPLATION OR DISCUSSION:

1. Review the *Webster's 1828 Dictionary* definition of sin.

2. What is always the cause of corruption of a person and a nation?

3. Dr. Langdon said, "for the sins of (who).................................. God may suffer the best government to be corrupted or entirely dissolved."

4. Dr. Langdon continued by saying: "nothing but .................................. can give good

ground to hope" for restoration and for God to raise up "wise and good men" to serve in government.

5. If "a general reformation" had taken place in Judah – which eventually did after judgment – what did Dr. Langdon indicate would be the good results?

   ..................................................................................................................

6. Did the clergy descriptions of the degenerated state of Judah, Israel, and even America then also describe the United States today? Are we in an even worse condition?

   ..................................................................................................................

7. What is God looking for before He is willing to restore a nation?

   ..................................................................................................................

8. What did Dr. Morse identify as the common, or shared, foundation of true religion and good government?

   ..................................................................................................................

9. Is it necessary to restore both true religion and the Church, as well as righteousness and justice in government, for a nation to be restored?

   ..................................................................................................................

## SERMON OUTLINE SUGGESTION:

1. What is always the cause of corruption of a person and a nation?
2. What are some of our national sins that are bringing God's judgment upon us?
3. What is God looking for in us before He is willing to restore us and our nation?

# EPILOGUE & STEPS
# OF RESTORATION

Dr. Jedidiah Morse and other clergy accurately described not only where the battle was in his day, but where it is today. Christianity and our constitutional forms of government are being assaulted, "subverted and overthrown." The foundations of our nation are being destroyed before our eyes. Like Dr. Morse, I "am compelled to sound the alarm, and I will do it, so far as GOD shall enable me." There is hope for restoration and a good future, but only in the LORD God, and only from Him through the clergy, the Church, and restoration of the nobility and leadership of men.

## State of Our Nation Today

I'd like to share a dream I had a few years ago. In that dream, I saw a great city in the United States with many buildings of varying heights. At first I was standing on a sidewalk in the downtown area. Everything looked normal, and people were walking, going into and coming out of the buildings. But then I was taken underneath the surface, and it looked like a dark, endless, one-level cavern, like an underground garage with just enough pillars still in place to hold up the buildings above. I saw explosive detonations, here and there, near and far, destroying most of the support structures of the buildings. The people above were unaware of the explosions occurring directly below them. Yet the destruction continued so that the city would eventually, suddenly, collapse within its own giant sinkhole, for its foundations had been destroyed. I believe this is a picture of the USA (and perhaps every other nation) today, and what has been going on in our nations for at least a century.

What exactly is the state of the United States today? We are a sinful people! Among us we have rampant immorality and adultery, rape, idolatry, the innocent bloodshed of more than 65 million babies by abortion, widespread broken marriage covenants and family breakups, racism, violence, murders, thefts, corruption, lawlessness, homosexuality, LGBTQ, and transgenderism. Millions of church-affiliated citizens have aborted their babies, and millions choose public officials, legislators, and judges who stand for policies antithetical to the Christian faith, morality, the sanctity of human life, and truth. We are self-destructing our nation.

Most clergy and Christians are highly reluctant to speak on any of these issues. As a nation, we have forgotten and rejected the God who gives life and liberty, in whom our forefathers believed. We have rejected the influence of Christianity in our public education, culture, and government. As the influence of the clergy and Christianity has diminished in our nation, so has our virtue, liberty, happiness, justice, peace, and good order.

## Can the Nation and its Good Foundations be Restored?

"If the foundations are destroyed, what can the righteous do" (Psalm 11:3)? We can rebuild the nation by rebuilding its foundations. But can we just decide to rebuild and do so successfully? No, that won't work. Why? Because we are a sinful people, and there is a Living God to whom we are accountable. To rebuild the nation, we must restore the fear and reverence of The LORD and our faith in Him, and then rebuild our foundations.

> The LORD is in His holy temple; the LORD's throne is in heaven; His eyes behold, His eyelids test the sons of men. The LORD tests the righteous and the wicked, and the one who loves violence His soul hates. Upon

the wicked He will rain snares; fire and brimstone
and burning wind will be the portion of their cup.
For the LORD is righteous, He loves righteousness;
the upright will behold His face (Psalm 11:4-7).

"The LORD is righteous, He loves righteousness"; His "throne
is in heaven." So how can we be restored to Him, to The Righteous
One? In the Bible is recorded the everlasting promise the LORD made
to King Solomon and Israel – a promise that He has also fulfilled
for Christians in any nation who responded rightly to Him as He
prescribed:

> Then the LORD appeared to Solomon at night and
> said to him, "I have heard your prayer . . . If I shut up
> the heavens so that there is no rain, or if I command
> the locust to devour the land, or if I send pestilence
> among My people, and My people who are called by
> My name humble themselves and pray and seek My
> face and turn from their wicked ways, then I will hear
> from heaven, will forgive their sin and will heal their
> land" (2 Chronicles 7:12-14).

God loves the world – all peoples, all nations – with His
unchanging, unfailing, everlasting love, by which He "gave His only
begotten Son, that whoever believes in Him should not perish, but have
eternal life" (John 3:16). Jesus Christ came, suffered, was crucified,
and rose "from the dead . . . that repentance for forgiveness of sins
would be proclaimed in His name to all the nations" (Luke 24:46-
47). It is our sin that separates us from God, both individually and as
a nation. Only if we repent of our sins, personally and nationally, can
we receive "forgiveness of sins" (1 John 1:8-10). Otherwise, we will
be subject to His judgments, which come in many forms, including
plagues, financial problems, corrupt governments, and attacks by
enemies. We cannot rebuild the foundations of our nation unless

we first face God, are honest with Him and each other about our national sins, and humbly confess them before Him. If we will do so, then we can be confident that He will give grace and power to once again become a virtuous and self-governing people, and wisdom in ordering our society.

What will it take to restore the United States of America? What will it take to restore your nation? Will rebellion, lawlessness, violence, riots, and foreigners overtake our cities and towns? Will another nation take us captive, or terrorists wreak destruction? Will we have a civil war and destroy one another? What will it take before we are finally willing to humble ourselves before Almighty God? What will it take for us to voluntarily return and ask Him to forgive us, change us and restore us?

## Steps to Restoration

The first steps toward restoration must include the following:

1. Clergy: take up your mantels as shepherd leaders of the church and community (for some, also your state or nation), and be strong and courageous, with wisdom and understanding, like the clergy did during the 1700s.
2. Clergy and Christian leaders: lead God's people in awareness and repentance for personal, church, community and national sins, and lead days of prayer, humiliation and fasting before the LORD.
3. God's people: respond rightly to the Spirit of God working and leading through His shepherds, in humbling yourselves personally and corporately during such days, turning from sin, and renewing your minds.
4. Men: be restored in your true identity, and take up your mantels of authority and responsibility, remembering God and His Word, and loving, honoring, leading, and protecting

170

your wife and children, and also leading well in your roles at church and work.

5. Women: be restored in your true identity, and take up your mantels of authority and responsibility, receiving and remembering God and His Word, and respecting, honoring and loving your husband, loving and nurturing your children, being open to receive, give, and nurture life, and leading or serving well in all your other noble roles.

6. Clergy and Christians: become Christ-like, faithful, virtuous people.

7. Clergy and God's people in every sphere: become students, thinkers, and practitioners of the Scriptures, knowing and upholding the Word of God, and His design and will also evident in nature, as the foundations for truth in every area of life, public policy, and government.

To be a virtuous people, we must fear the LORD, hate every form of evil, whether in ourselves or others—not hating ourselves or others, but only the sin—for the "fear of the LORD is to hate evil" (Proverbs 8:13). A virtuous people are a God-fearing, moral, honest, law-abiding, and self-governing people. Such a people voluntarily do what is right because they fear and love the LORD. These qualities in the people are essential to restoring, establishing and sustaining righteous, just, free and limited governments.

To restore the good foundations, some of the essential building blocks that fit within the first steps above (with some repetition) are evident in the wisdom of the clergy preserved for us and future generations in each chapter of this book.

1. Clergyman, take up your mantel as a spiritual leader and shepherd of God's people and your community, and perhaps your state and the nation, proclaiming and teaching the truth – including by teaching on each topic addressed in this book (e.g., a weekly series), the sanctity of human life and

evil of abortion [see the Global Life Campaign and Abortion Worldwide Report information on the last page of this book], and other critical matters of personal and public concern (Chapter 1).

2. Clergy and Christians, with reverence, respect, and boldness, acknowledge Almighty God, Jesus Christ as Savior and LORD, and His goodness and sovereignty, privately and publicly (Chapter 2).

3. Clergy, Christians, and Jews, acknowledge and obey God by keeping the LORD's Day or the Sabbath Day holy each week; and by keeping a clear conscience and good relationships through confessing known sins and reconciliation before worship; and by closing all non-essential businesses on that Day each week (Chapter 2).

4. Restore recognition of liberty as a gift of God amongst God's people, in education, and publicly; and the understanding that virtue, morality, and self-government are essential to preserve a righteous, just and free nation (Chapter 3).

5. Teach the truth – in your homes, churches, schools, colleges, seminaries, libraries, museums, public – about the founding of the American Colonies, including the influence of clergy and Christianity, and that America was settled as an asylum for religious and civil liberty (Chapter 4).

6. Teach the truth about freedoms of mind, conscience and religion, and protect these unalienable God-given rights for present and future generations (Chapter 5).

7. Teach the truth about the distinction between sins and crimes to restrain civil government from punishing people unjustly, but encourage them to render justice for criminal actions (Chapter 6).

8. Teach the truth about the realms of religion and government, of the Church and the state, of the duties owed to God and duties owed to man (Chapter 7).

9.  Teach the true meaning of "no establishment of religion" (Chapter 8).

10. Teach how to identify and why to choose good rulers (Chapter 9).

11. Teach faithful submission and obedience to good rulers and good laws, and respectful disobedience to tyrants, and that doing both is essential for complete obedience to God (Chapter 10).

12. Teach the truth about the American Revolution, its purpose, and that its cause was just and blessed by God with success (Chapter 11).

13. Teach the truth about the sin of slavery, including that it was the cause of the Civil War and racism, yet how God worked miraculously and redemptively to free the slaves, and how national repentance is still necessary today to end racism (Chapter 12); and,

14. Teach the truth about the cause of corruption of a nation – sin – but how God has already provided a method of personal and national restoration through Jesus (Chapter 13).

## Final Thoughts

God set aside America as an asylum of liberty, a sanctuary for religious and civil liberty under God, where every person has inherent worth, dignity, and equality, regardless of their national origin or color. Satan, the enemy of our souls, has sought to thwart God's purpose by bringing materialism, greed, slavery, racism, discrimination, rampant immorality, abortion, divorce, etc. Even so, God's purpose for our nation can still be restored if we will return to Him. If we truly humble ourselves before God and genuinely repent of all our personal and national sins, and turn from all our wicked ways, then He will restore us and His purpose for our nation. If clergy and believers in Jesus Christ once again become salt to preserve, light to guide, and "the pillar and support of the truth" (1 Timothy 3:15), then there is good hope for the future of the United States of America.

God enabled the clergy and Christians of the 1700s to build a free, united and glorious nation, which we have nearly torn down. If we will once again choose the LORD as our God, He is able to restore our liberty, unity and glory. For "Blessed is the nation whose God is the LORD, the people whom He has chosen for His own inheritance" (Psalm 33:12).

# INDEX OF CLERGY IN BOOK

# GENERAL INDEX

# GLOBAL LIFE CAMPAIGN

The author, Thomas W. Jacobson, formed the Global Life Campaign in late 2011.

**VISION**: Abortion is no more!

**MISSION:**

1. **REMEMBER** the Bible as the unchanging foundation for truth in all of life;
2. **RESEARCH** abortion worldwide and document the Greatest Genocide;
3. **INSPIRE** the Church to be "the pillar and support of the Truth" and defend life;
4. **ADVOCATE** for the preborn among the nations; and
5. **SERVE** movements to end abortion in every nation.

https://GLC.life

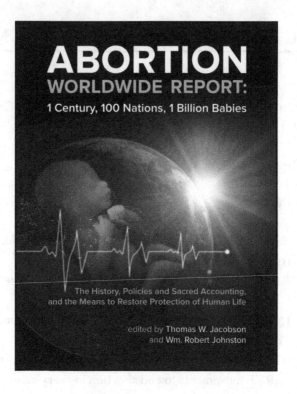

**ABORTION**
**WORLDWIDE REPORT:**
1 Century, 100 Nations, 1 Billion Babies

The History, Policies and Sacred Accounting,
and the Means to Restore Protection of Human Life

edited by Thomas W. Jacobson
and Wm. Robert Johnston

The **Abortion Worldwide Report (AWR)** is the culmination of 40 years of research by Thomas W. Jacobson and Wm. Robert Johnston, Ph.D. (GLC Publications, 2018; updated version coming in 2024).

**Means of Restoration** (part I)

- 8 universal truths: sanctity human life (part I);
- Scientific & medical evidence (part I);
- 7 universal principles: human rights (part I);
- 7 universal principles: civil government (part I);
- 5 universal principles: law and rule of law (part I);
- Biblical analyses of innocent bloodshed & accountability to God for individuals and nations (part VIII);
- Truth & hope for repentance, forgiveness, & restoration (parts VIII & IX).

**History, Policies & Abortion Data** (parts II – VII, X, addendums)

- History: nations protecting life, 1800s—2024 (2024 edition).
- Nations authorizing abortion, 1920—2024.
- Reasons women give for having abortions.
- National policies of 196 nations plus territories.
- Data sources; reliable methods for missing data.
- Sacred Accounting: nearly 1.4 billion reported abortions, 1921—2023, for 110 nations and 35 territories.
- World and regional maps; national graphs; tables; and lists.
- Major findings (including Greatest Genocide).
- Data sources, country, and general indexes.

Available at: www.GLCPublications.com.
English: print, eBook & iBook;
Spanish: eBook or iBook.

Printed in the United States
by Baker & Taylor Publisher Services